# Epic Marriage

*Every Marriage Has a Purpose—*
*Discover Yours*

*Andrew J. Werley*

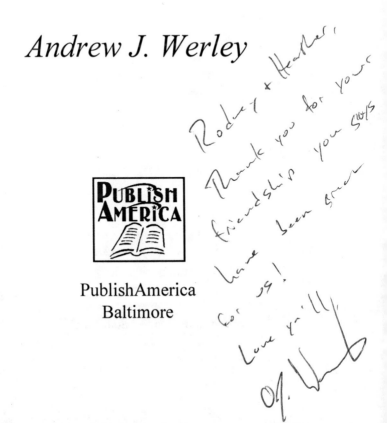

**PublishAmerica**
Baltimore

First printing

ISBN: 1-4241-6325-0
PUBLISHED BY PUBLISHAMERICA, LLLP
www.publishamerica.com
Baltimore

Printed in the United States of America

Dedicated to Angie, my inspiring, loving, epic bride. Thanks for being my anchor and inspiration to pursue God's purpose.

*Angie and I would like to thank all the people who helped shape us as a couple and made this book possible:*

*Thanks to parents: Mike, Betty, Gary, Yvonne, Cora; brothers and sisters: Alisha, Cory and Suzanne. You have been great cheerleaders through this process. Thanks to Pastor Jim and Marcy Carter for investing in our marriage and our pre-marriage. Thanks to Terry and Jan Graham for encouraging our marriage every day.*

*Thanks to Chris Wommack for painfully working through my first draft. You are a saint; thanks for your writing insight and wisdom. Thanks to Abigail Criner for taking my picture. Thanks to Carrie Schneider for the incredible art work, and thanks to all of our young married friends at First Baptist Woodway for your loving support.*

*Thanks for the background music while I wrote, Derek Webb's* I See Things Upside Down, *Andrew Peterson, Passion Worship Band (99-06), Sarah Groves, Ottmar Leibert, John Mayer, Shane Barnard, Jack Johnson, Coldplay, and of course Miles Davis'* Kind of Blue.

*Thanks to Hollywood for the epics that inspire us to be more.*

# Contents

# Chapter 1
# Epics

I don't watch R-rated movies. I know it sounds very old fashioned, but every time I see an R movie, it seems to offend me. As with most commitments, it is good to have an out sometimes. I noticed by committing not to see R movies, I was avoiding a lot of offensive stuff, but I was missing many great stories. So, I developed a new standard for the R movies I would see. I only watch epics. I deemed it appropriate and even necessary to see an R movie if it was considered epic-worthy. I defined an epic as a movie that had an incredible and possibly life-changing story line. My hope was that by seeing the epic despite the risk of exposure to nudity, violence, or evil, I would have my life course altered for having seen the story. Finally, I could see *Braveheart, The Passion, Gladiator*, and *Black Hawk Down.*

Epics are usually powerfully realistic, so realistic you can watch the story and begin to identify with the actors, their decisions, and their consequences. You come to a point in the production that you desire the best for the people acting in the film. When the movie is over, you sit back, consider your life and the decisions you are making and hope that you too will end up being in your own epic. At the end of *Braveheart,* I wanted to be a catalyst and hero. After *The Passion,* I wept and cried out to God because my sin caused His blood and pain. After

*Gladiator,* I wanted to find more courage to do the things that are right no matter what. I had to watch *Black Hawk Down* and *When We Were Soldiers* in segments. They were too difficult to watch at once. When I finally finished both of these movies, I appreciated all that my dad did as a Marine in the Vietnam War for me and the United States. Now I call my dad every Memorial Day and Veterans' Day and verbally thank him for fighting for my freedom.

Epics are bloody. They contain scenes that are realistic in nature and so does your life. Every day you make a decision to live life as normal or to engage in a fight; the fight for what is real and the fight to be a part of something bigger than you! In the pages to come, I want to inspire your fight for your marriage to be epic. To be exposed to the blood, the tears, and the reality so that one day your marriage will be considered a story that changes lives.

This book is not a typical marriage book. As I strolled through the shelves of marriage books in my local Christian bookstore, I noticed books full of ways to help you meet each other's needs, unlock secret passions, endless steps to having a healthy marriage and more. I want to introduce to you the truth that your marriage is not only about needs. I also think there is more to a healthy marriage than just having great communication skills and a nightly devotion together. Needs are important, good communication is helpful and a nightly devotion is healthy, but God did not design and propose your marriage to do just those things.

The problem with some marriage self-help books is that they promote the idea that if these things are not present in your marriage, it is an excuse or valid reason to call off the marriage. I hear too often, "She is not meeting my *needs* so this is just not working out," or, "We are holier when we're not with each other. God must not want us together." The standard couples are gauging their marriages by temporal factors like needs and feelings versus eternal factors like God and Salvation. God did not give to humanity marriage just to meet needs. He had a greater purpose in mind when He first gave marriage to Adam and Eve. He said that they were to have lots of children and after the fall, He tells them He is going to use the seed of the woman to bring salvation to the world. In other words, God planned from the beginning to use marriage as a tool to bring salvation to humanity. Paul continues this notion by affirming that a marriage centered on Christ will reveal the "mystery" of salvation. Jesus Christ is the greatest epic figure of all time. No one event in all of history compares to the bloody life-changing sacrifice of Jesus Christ. He embodies the word "epic." An Epic Marriage before Christ is a tool God used to bring Christ into the world through the seed of Abraham. An Epic Marriage after the resurrection is a marriage that reflects the mystery of oneness with God through Christ's death.

This book is about your marriage revealing the mystery. I hope to encourage you to center your marriage on Christ so that you will reveal the oneness that we can have with God when we trust in Christ as Savior. The revelation of Jesus Christ and the events of the cross contain the elements of the greatest epic of all time. In God's ultimate wisdom and mercy, He has decided to include marriage as an essential component to revealing His epic.

This book is broken into two main sections. The first section is how marriage fit into God's plan of bringing Christ to the world. It systemizes and applies God's use of key couples in the Old Testament included in the heritage of Christ's earthly ancestors. After Christ's birth, death and resurrection, the story continues. The second section is living out Christ's story today.

God wants to reveal the Gospel of Jesus Christ to people for the first time and it is His plan for your marriage to be a tool in His post-resurrection epic.

When a couple agrees to focus their marriage on revealing Christ, their marriage has a renewed focus and purpose. Instead of focusing inwardly, they begin to think outwardly. Likewise, instead of thinking the purpose of marriage is to bring you happiness, you discover that the purpose of you marriage is bring God glory. Now trials and disappointments become epic opportunities to reveal Christ and not opportunities to give up. If you decide to embrace the principles in this book, you will begin a journey into a God-centered, Christ-revealing marriage as you discover the deeper, more satisfying purpose for your marriage.

As we continue, things are going to get bloody. You will need to consider how your marriage can make some positive changes and you may need to expose real sins to God's light. I think you will find that although this topic sounds nebulous, as you read on it will become not only practical, but also achievable. Achievable in the sense that by the grace of Jesus Christ, you can have a marriage that is intentional about focusing on God and revealing Christ to a world that has yet to see Him. Welcome to the epic.

# Chapter 2
# Epic Model

## Adam and Eve: The Model

*Then the LORD God said, "It is not good for the man to be alone; I will make him a helper suitable for him." Out of the ground the LORD God formed every beast of the field and every bird of the sky, and brought them to the man to see what he would call them; and whatever the man called a living creature, that was its name. The man gave names to all the cattle, and to the birds of the sky, and to every beast of the field, but for Adam there was not found a helper suitable for him. So the LORD God caused a deep sleep to fall upon the man, and he slept; then He took one of his ribs and closed up the flesh at that place. The LORD God fashioned into a woman the rib which He had taken from the man, and brought her to the man.*

*The man said,*

*"This is now bone of my bones, and flesh of my flesh;*
*She shall be called Woman,*
*Because she was taken out of Man."*

*For this reason a man shall leave his father and his mother, and be joined to his wife; and they shall become one flesh. And the man and his wife were both naked and were not ashamed (Genesis 2:18-25).*

# No Man Is an Island

Who wrote the phrase "No man is an island"? John Donne? John Milton? John F. Kennedy? Jon Bon Jovi? Jon Bon Jovi. Too easy. And, if I may say so, a complete load of bollocks. In my opinion, all men are islands. And what's more, now's the time to be one! This is an island age. A hundred years ago, you had to depend on other people. No one had TV, CDs, DVDs or videos…or home espresso makers. Actually, they didn't have anything cool. Whereas now, you see, you can make yourself a little island paradise. With the right supplies and the right attitude, you can be sun-drenched, tropical, a magnet for young Swedish tourists.[1]

The movie *About a Boy* begins with Will (Hugh Grant) rationalizing his egocentric lifestyle, concluding that he is capable of being an "island," self-sufficient in every way having no need for anyone (except Swedish tourists). The movie ends (if you haven't seen it yet, you may want to skip this paragraph) with Will in a relationship and his young protege saying, "You need backup." The way I saw it, Will and I both had backup. It's like that thing he told me Jon Bon Jovi said, "No man is an island." *About a Boy* is a story of the truth that we are all created with an unquenchable need for a partner, backup, or someone with whom to experience life. God divinely created men and women with this need. He uses this need to draw us into a relationship with Him. He fulfills this need in many ways and most often it is through the gift of marriage.

When God designed marriage, He had two major purposes in mind. The first purpose is having children. God told the first married couple that they were to be fruitful and multiply. The second category God had in mind when He created marriage was humanity's need for a relationship with Him. When couples commit to being a part of a godly legacy through children and to revealing Christ to humanity, they will meet each other's needs. Men and women come into marriage with a different set of needs; for example a love language or the need for appreciation, acceptance and affection. Meeting these needs helps a marriage be fruitful. Both the husband and the wife have a role in meeting one another's needs. Nevertheless, needs are not the sole purpose of marriage. Needs are only met when couples commit to living out what God's purpose is for marriage. With the first marriage in the Bible, God has provided an example of marriage that not only meets the temporal needs of a man and a woman, but also more importantly meets the eternal needs of humanity.

For centuries, the Jewish nation most often considered one couple to be the model for marriage. You may even know their story. However, you may not have considered their story to have much of an impact on yours. History and the Bible refer to them as Adam and Eve. For most of us, the first things that come to mind in hearing those names are a fig leaf and an apple tree. It is true they are the ones that messed up paradise for the rest of humanity. But before the great apple tree incident something beautiful occurred: the first marriage. What made this particular marriage so beautiful was that God created it before the fall of humanity and, even better, God laid out for the rest of us a model by which we can have a purposeful marriage.

## Man

In the book of Genesis, we have the account of the first man, the first woman and the first marriage. It is here that we begin to see God's design for man's roles in life and marriage. Before the first wife comes onto the scene, Adam is given some assignments. In Genesis chapter 2, verse 15, God commands Adam to work the Garden of Eden. Even in paradise, man has a job to do. God gives Adam the gardener's job. This is work, but it is pretty cushy. It's work before the curse, so no ground is fighting back at him when he tries to dig, no thorn bushes are there to cut him when he is clearing out brush, and probably every fruit he picked up and every flower he smelled was perfect—no blemishes, nothing rotten. It was the perfect job.

The second activity assigned to Adam, before he receives his wife, is worship. It looks different. God does not tell him to go to church, the temple, or the synagogue. However, God is calling him to worship.

*The LORD God commanded the man, saying, "From any tree of the garden you may eat freely;*
*but from the tree of the knowledge of good and evil you shall not eat, for in the day that you eat from it you will surely die" (Genesis 2:16-17).*

This is Adam's and eventually Eve's opportunity to live a lifestyle that worships God. In the tree of knowledge, there is a divine opportunity presented to Adam. God is telling Adam, "For the rest of your days here in paradise, everything will be easy, but you will have one thing you cannot do." By not doing this one thing, Adam chooses freely every day to follow God and to trust Him for provision beyond what the tree of knowledge promises. This decision to follow God is one of the ways we worship Him. Worship is more than singing songs on Sunday mornings. Worship is fighting temptation, working hard for your boss, loving your wife, and loving your neighbor as yourself. When we choose to follow God's commands, we are pledging our allegiance to His provision and His will. That is worship. Paul says it like this in the book of Romans:

*Therefore I urge you, brethren, by the mercies of God, to present your bodies a living and holy sacrifice, acceptable to God, which is your spiritual service of worship.*

*And do not be conformed to this world, but be transformed by the renewing of your mind, so that you may prove what the will of God is, that which is good and acceptable and perfect (Romans 12:1-2).*

Paul says when we choose, by mercy, to follow God and transform our inward desires from what is not of God, we offer up our lives as a sacrifice in worship to God.

God is still asking humanity to do these two things: work and worship. Your work is as ordained as worship, and I will even venture to say that your work is worship. By now you may be asking, "Why all this talk about man's purpose in the garden? I thought this was a marriage book?" I am glad you asked.

## Woman

God tells Adam that He sees his need for a helper. Next God creates animals. Now put yourself in Adam's shoes for a minute. God tells you He is going to make for you a helper and the next thing you know God is walking livestock in front of you. The whole time you have to be wondering, which one of these is for me? This is exactly how I feel when I walk into the Gap. I head to our local mall, walk by all the department stores and stroll into the Gap. Then an overwhelming anxiety hits me and I wonder, "Which side is the guy side?" If there are no skirts out front, I am lost. On every side, I see pastel polos and blue jeans. Eventually, I pick a side and hope that I'm right.

After naming all the animals, still no suitable helper is found for Adam. Luckily, Adam doesn't have to pick one. God puts Adam under a "divine sleep" and takes from him a rib. God uses this rib to create a helper suitable for Adam.

I don't mean to read too much into the text, but I wonder, "Why did God use a rib?" God could have chosen any portion of Adam to make Eve. God could have even chosen to make Eve the same way He created Adam. Yet God chose a rib from Adam. Scripture never reveals the mystery of the rib. There is the implication that the man and the woman are meant to be together. Legendary theologian and Bible scholar Matthew Henry weaves beautifully the possible spirit behind God using a rib, "not made out of his head to top him, not out of his feet to be trampled upon by him, but out of his side to be equal with him, under his arm to be protected, and near his heart to be beloved."[2] I think that is a beautiful way to look at why God used man's rib to make woman. Using the rib does say that woman's position in creation and marriage is different from that of the beasts and of man. She does not belong in a barn and she has equal footing with man concerning her relationship with God. Yet she is still under his stewardship.

## The Wedding Day

I wonder if it was like the movies when Adam finally wakes up to find God and Eve standing together in front of him. You know, just like when the hero is knocked out risking his life for the girl, and as he is coming to everything is blurry. He sees God, recognizes His shape, but who is that standing with Him? "I've never seen anything like *it*! It is so unique, what is this thumping in my chest?" As God helps Adam to his feet, Eve takes a step back peacefully to give him room to find his balance. God announces, "Adam, this is for you. Together you will help each other to work the earth and worship me."

Then something unique happens. Classic poetry erupts from Adam's heart when he experiences love at first sight, "This is now bone of my bones and flesh of my flesh." Adam sees the connection, "I was created in God's image and she comes from me." Next, Adam does what God has asked him to do with everything He creates. Adam names her. "She shall be called *issah*, because she was taken out of *is*." (*Issah* means woman and *is* means man in Hebrew. Nothing special about it, but the poetry is easier to see this way). "She is special; she is an extension of me and just as God called me to tend the garden I will tend to her."

Creation is complete. With the man as the lead steward, he and the woman will be stewards of all that God has entrusted to them and worship Him in the process. Next, God is going to lay out before Adam and Eve how He desires a man and a woman to spend the rest of their lives together.

## I Now Pronounce You, Man and Woman

It is important to realize that Adam's new wife is Adam's new responsibility. In our culture, this concept is very unpopular, especially if you live outside the Bible Belt. It seems that more and more men and women are misunderstanding the importance of men being the lead stewards in their homes. This is a privilege man receives when he marries the woman of his dreams. Like Adam, God is now entrusting her heart to him. He is to cultivate and care for it, just as God had employed Adam to care for the garden.

I can honestly say in over ten years of ministry I have never met a woman who said she didn't want her husband to help her become a better worshiper of God. Angie has never come to me and said, "Babe, I am my own woman and I don't want you to meet my needs, to support me, or be on my team anymore." What I have seen are men who do nothing.

Men so often say and do nothing when it comes to leading in the home. I think this is because they have no reliable example. Today many men grow up in homes with moms and dads who have never prayed together or gone to church together. Many men never had a male spiritual leader in the home. At least, that was my experience.

I was a leader in college, in my Young Life club, in my church. But when I married Angie, I didn't know the first thing about leading in marriage. To make matters more intimidating, I married a woman who was not only drop-dead gorgeous, but she also had been a Christian longer than me. She was a leader in a thriving youth group as a high school student and a leader in her college ministry. She woke up every morning to her dad reading his Bible in their living room. Now somehow I was supposed to offer this woman leadership.

I imagine when this fear hits any guy, unless he is pre-equipped by parents, a pastor or role-model of some kind, he will respond the way I did: do nothing. The problem with that response is your marriage will always miss your leadership. It will float through the sea of time aimlessly never having experienced the direction and fullness that come from having a man to tend and cultivate the home spiritually.

I have a garden. It takes up one-fourth of our backyard. It has an oleander, garlic, iris, lilies, roses, and native Texas flowers. There is a stone path through the center to a bench swing. It is a beautiful place, especially in the spring. As a garden owner, I realize I have to tend the garden. If it is covered in weeds, it no longer serves its purpose. The garden is no longer a beautiful focal point in our backyard and it becomes an eyesore. To be honest, I would rather rent a tiller, tear the whole thing out, and put in a pool. We don't have the money for a pool, so I won't do that. However, when the garden is in full bloom, it's worth the hours I have spent cultivating it. That is leadership in marriage. At its core, it is cultivating your marriage so it can bloom. Some seasons it may be dormant, dry or even ugly, but keep working at it and eventually it will bloom again. I really believe God has designed men to initiate this purpose. He designed us to protect and lead our homes. Not in some macho Rambo way, for spiritual leadership is deeper than that. It has very little to do with the size of your biceps (that may help though) and everything to do with your personal relationship with God.

So the secret to leading your home is having a great relationship with God and the secret to a great relationship with God is worship. So if you are doing one (worship) the other will follow (leading in the home). The problem is so many men look to excel at the first task of creation—work, and ignore the second—worship. So at the end of the day there is nothing to offer the family except the fruits of your labor, not the fruits of your worship.

Leading my wife does not mean changing her, fixing her, or making her holy. Leading my wife is watering her with prayer, giving her nourishment by sharing something God taught me in His Word or in an experience, and enjoying her beauty while listening to what God is doing in her life. My first job as the spiritual leader of my wife is to cultivate her with the resources God has given me.

What is my primary job as the spiritual leader of my wife and home? To keep God at the center. If all men would make it their responsibility to keep God at the center of their marriage, I believe they would be the spiritual leaders God intended.

My advice to men concerning leadership is to learn how to worship. Worship is song and dance. Sing even if you can't, and live like you are accountable to someone other than yourself. Realize that the more you spend time with God the more tools you will have to keep Him at the center of your marriage. In the pages to come, I hope to shed more light on what it means to be the spiritual leader of your home, to avoid putting the temporal things of this world at the center of your marriage, and to keep God first.

## Stuck to You

*For this reason a man shall leave his father and mother and be joined to his wife; and they shall become one flesh (Genesis 2:24).*

Another beautiful characteristic of an Epic Marriage is becoming one flesh. For years I thought this was just about sex. While that is an obvious factor, I don't think that is all God is expressing with this passage.

First, you leave Dad and Mom. *Forsake* may be a more accurate translation. Cut them off. It sounds harsh, but it illustrates the creation of a new family unit. Mom and Dad are still Mom and Dad, but when you get married, you have started a new family unit. You have your own home, you have your own priorities, your own decisions, your own consequences, and you have each other. Being joined together is beautifully portrayed in the Hebrew as *stuck to each other*. It is not like a Lego set where plastic pieces are clipped to each other only to be taken apart later to create something different. *Stuck to each other* is more like you were once male and female, but now you are Siamese twins.

In some conjoined (this is the appropriate term for what used to be Siamese) twin cases the twins share a heart. These twins are called thoracopagus twins.[3] When surgeons have attempted to separate thoracopagus twins, they have a 0% success rate. In other words, when twins that share a heart are separated, they always die. I think there is a picture of marriage in heart-conjoined twins. His blood becomes her blood, her skin becomes his skin, and his feelings become her feelings. If for some reason you try to separate the two, you will never be the same. You will always be related, but never be the same, and there is a 0% chance of surviving a separating surgery. It is so devastating to try to separate what God has joined together that it becomes obvious they were never meant to be separated.

The risk of separating what God has joined is rarely worth it. I know I am supposed to say *never*, but I said *rarely*. The fact of the matter is there are some extreme cases that I would say, "Surgery is worth the risk." Even then, godly counsel from a trusted pastor or Christian counselor is critical before you take action to leave a spouse. In most cases, it is not worth the risk and the damage is greater than the reward. Forgiving my spouse for sinful failure brings more glory to God and is more rewarding than separating what God has joined together.

When the Bible says, "They were stuck together and became one flesh" it is saying marriage is a gift of kinship with another person. God is beginning a new family unit through your union. A new legacy will begin through your family. Becoming one flesh is a beautiful union that has making love involved, but at its deepest core is the godly union of a couple to the point that their hearts and lives could not survive without being joined together.

# Naked

"And the man and his wife were both naked and were not ashamed." English translates shame as guilt, but freedom from guilt was not the issue. Free from concern, imperfection and content with God's provision is a more accurate description of what is happening in the garden. Free and unaware may be a better way to say it. It comes along with being one in the flesh. I actually think that this is more of the sex part.

When I worked with youth, one of the areas in which I really wanted to see teenagers succeed was with their sexual purity. I wanted with all my heart for students to be spared the burden of being sexually impure when they got married. My desire was for every girl and every guy to walk into the security of their honeymoon night knowing that neither one of them knew what they were doing. In addition, because of their love for each other, innocence, and their unity in God, they could have complete security in being naked together.

The first man and the first woman could be naked and unaware because their marriage was not based on physical attractiveness (not a bad thing, it just won't last). We are to be naked and unaware in marriage, content in the provision of the Father. Naked and unashamed is the security offered in a healthy God-centered, epic-focused marriage. This marriage allows for the husband and the wife to be real, to be personal, and to fail sometimes knowing they will still find acceptance in the one with whom God has joined. Naked and unashamed says that you are at the center of God's will in your relationship with your spouse.

# Epic Needs, Epic Purpose

Once a week I meet with a friend who is a professor at a local university. We usually run along the Brazos River from his campus to a local city park. We talk about life, theology, church, and anything from Civil War history to why it is so hot in Texas. One time I invited him to join me on a trail run through a local park with rugged, rolling miles of mountain bike and hiking trails. It is shaded and padded with dirt and the terrain offers a nice challenge. One day we were coming up the backside of the hill after running for about thirty minutes in the Texas heat. We were still twenty minutes away from our cars and I was exhausted, but my buddy, who is older but in far better shape, just kept running up the hill. I told him, "The only reason I am still running is because you are!" There have been many times in running the race of ministry and Christianity that I have turned to my wife and said, "The only reason I am still running is because you are." To which she lovingly responds, "I know; pick up the pace, fat boy!"

What makes marriage great is having someone with whom to laugh, to struggle, and to share the work and worship of life. God has called us all to work and worship and He created your spouse to be a partner in work and worship. When a marriage is committed to working for the Lord and worshiping God, it is epic.

Later Eve and Adam will eat from the tree of knowledge. God will curse humankind for his disobedience and He will set the epic in motion. When God curses humanity, He begins by cursing Satan who is in the form of a serpent in the Garden. To the serpent God says:

*And I will put enmity between you and the woman,*
*And between your seed and her seed;*
*He shall bruise you on the head and you shall bruise him on*
*the heel (Genesis 3:15).*

Scholars consider this passage to be the first messianic prophecy in the Old Testament. Before the tree had been placed in the garden, Jesus was placed on the cross. God had already claimed victory over the failure of Adam and Eve in the garden. Genesis claims that the seed of woman will defeat Satan. God is going to use the seed of marriage through Abraham to bring His son into the world. The stage has been set for the greatest epic of all. Adam and Eve are the first of a long line of characters essential to God's epic plan of revealing salvation.

## Perfect Model

In conclusion, Scripture provides for humanity through the example of the first husband and the first wife, God's ordained basis for marital order. First, God created man and gave him leadership over creation. In addition, God required from man his worship. Out of man, God created woman. She was created out of the man, named by man, giving him the privilege of leading her while she shares in the stewardship of the creation and worship of God. In marriage, God causes two hearts to become one, and He will use the greater purposes of marriage (children and revealing salvation) to provide for the intimate needs of a man and a woman. Finally, God sets in motion His epic plan for marriage as a tool to bring humanity back into relationship with Him after the fall, through the death of His perfect son, Jesus Christ. In Adam and Eve, God provides a blueprint for marriage that will continue to transcend culture and time because of its fundamental expression of deep inner human qualities; nevermind the fact that God made us and designed marriage.

I must make it clear that I believe marriage is ordained to meet the specific needs of men and women, but a grander purpose for marriage remains. God is making an epic mosaic with tiles: blue, white, yellow, brown, green, crimson and many other colors. When every tile is set, the grand mosaic will reveal to all of humanity a sacrifice that will redeem us from darkness, death, and suffering. The sacrifice will provide light, life and healing through a relationship with God. The mosaic reveals Christ's epic death on the cross. His death is essential to humanity's fellowship and oneness with God the Father.

Without a relationship with Jesus the Savior, we can never know the Father and the Heavenly inheritance He has for us. I do not know why, it must be the romantic in me, but I am thankful that God used marriage to bring the Savior into the world. From Adam and Eve to Mary and Joseph, God proposed marriage and family as one of His tools for bringing salvation to the world. Young Mary, a descendant of Abraham, was a virgin when the Holy Spirit placed Christ in her womb. The significance of Abraham will be explained in the next chapter.

God tells us in Scripture that He is still using marriage. God still plans to use marriage to reveal His Son to humanity. The point of this book is to retell some of the marriage stories God used in His epic story leading up to the cross. Some of the couples are frail, chipped, and discolored, but God still chose to use them for His glory. The second point is to give you a passion to continue the epic with your marriage. My hope is that you will not only see your marriage as a tool God uses to meet your needs, but more importantly as a relationship designed and intended to reveal Christ.

## Discussion Questions with Your Spouse or Small Group

*Where do we look for model marriages?*

*Why is the choice not to eat from the tree of good and evil considered worship?*

*What are some of your daily personal worship choices?*

*Why do you think God used a rib from man to create woman?*

*Put flesh and bones on the model marriage. What does it look like every day? What are its characteristics?*

# Chapter 3
# Epic Faith

## Abraham and Sarah: Go and Believe

Imagine visually inhaling dozens of images of time right now. After Adam and Eve succumbed to temptation in the Garden of Eden, God cursed Satan, the ground and then He turned the hourglass. Time as we know it began. The sand swirls through the narrow knot racing towards the day when time ends. After the fall of man in the Garden of Eden, creation begins to evolve and construct societies. Adam and Eve's sons marry and descendants are added to the first man and woman. Hundreds of men, women and children now roam the earth, creating the wheel, discovering fire, buildings, medicine, and survival. Waiting for God's next move, man becomes fascinated with himself. He begins to worship himself and all the possible pleasures he can receive.

God makes a move. He asks Noah to build a boat for a society that had never seen rain. The boat is large. Every creature, great and small, two-by-two are loaded onto the boat, along with Noah and his family, as God cleanses the sinful earth with rain. The rains stop to reveal a break of sunshine and a rainbow. As the waters evaporate, man hits the ground running. Waiting for God's next move, man decides to build a large tower to see what God is doing in the Heavens. God is not threatened, but for humanity's own good, God divides them by languages and people groups. Time races as man waits for God's next move.

For the first time since the fall of man, we see God initiate humanity instead of responding to humanity. He finds a man drenched in a culture of multiple gods and idols; a society strapped by the fear of demons, witchcraft and omens; a man from Mesopotamia, a religious land rich with grains, fruits, vegetables, fish, oils, wine and silver. God chooses this one man for whatever reason to do two simple things: God asks Abram to "go and believe." God tells Abram to leave the wealth and false security of his land and go to a new land "that I will show you." God adds "believe" to "go." God makes a covenant with Abram based simply on Abram's belief. God opens the eyes of Abram to see that there is only one true God and that He is making His next move.

With the Abrahamic Covenant, God continues to develop His epic salvation. God plans to use the DNA of Abram as the legacy that will be Jesus the Christ. God promises Abram if he will go and believe, He will one day make him into a mighty nation that will bless all the families of the earth. Abram and his wife Sarai will go and they will believe, but they will have a few mishaps along the way. Mercifully, God uses the mishaps to bless and teach Abram and Sarai. In addition to blessing and teaching, God will keep His covenant with Abram.

## Dilemma and Joy

For some reason, the past few nights my son, Austin, has digressed from sleeping through the night to waking up at three in the morning, ready to eat. One morning in particular, Angie climbed back into bed just as I was getting up for my morning run. She was so tired that she asked me to stay and take care of Austin if he woke up. Honestly, I was a little bummed! That is the sacrifice of fatherhood. So I woke up, read in my Bible, ate some Grape-Nuts, and watched Sportscenter before I heard crying down the hall. I quickly walked to Austin's room, picked him up, and cradled him in my arms. He fell immediately back to sleep. It is amazing how secure he feels in my arms. It is like he melts right into me.

We went back to the living room and sat on the couch. In the silence, I was looking out at our garden in full bloom. I began to think about Abraham and Sarah. How God told them they were going to have a child, and they waited twenty-five years for Him to deliver. I looked down at my son sleeping in my arms, and began to remember his journey to existence.

Four and half years before, Angie and I had started trying to have kids. I say trying; it was really more not trying to not have kids. A year into the process, I took a position at another church and we moved. We realized a year had gone by and began to take aggressive steps towards conceiving a child. We started doing the biological tricks scientists tell you to do to get pregnant. *Any day now,* we thought. Another year went by and nothing. So we took things a step further. We talked to the OB/ GYN and began taking a low-dose medication. A few months later, we were pregnant! Then as fast as the pregnancy came, it was gone. We wept, prayed and wondered. Angie handled it extremely well. She and I both realized that God was in control of when, if ever, it was time for us to have kids. No one (not even us) was going to interfere with His plan. Three months later in April, we were pregnant again. With the exception of a little bed rest, it was an easy pregnancy (you should probably ask Angie about that, though).

Sometimes, I wonder how far we would have gone. Was there a point at which we were interfering with God's plan?

Were we forcing what we believed was His will? We both felt like we were going to be parents and we wanted kids, but maybe we were supposed to adopt. Hundreds of kids are born every day needing a home. The scenarios and ethical considerations are vast (too vast for this book). All I know is at some point we had to ask ourselves, *Is this God's will or ours?*

Abram and Sarai found themselves in a similar situation. To their advantage, God promised Abram land, children, and blessing. They must have felt tremendous pressure culturally. It was considered a curse not to have children. Children were essential to the day-to-day tasks of an agricultural society. In many ways, they were like 401k plans of the ancient world. Having children was insurance that someone was going to help take care of you when you couldn't work anymore. Yet Abram and Sarai, the chosen father and mother of God's people, were childless and elderly. Their story begins with one request, from God: "go and believe." Every time they wavered from faith or added to God's simple request, something tragic happened. Their story is a story of God's grace in the midst of poor decisions. A story of faith with which we can all identify.

## The Covenant

*Now the LORD said to Abram "Go forth from your country, and from your relatives and from your father's house, to the land which I will show you;*

*And I will make you a great nation and I will bless you, and make your name great; and so you shall be a blessing;*

*And I will bless those who bless you, and the one who curses you I will curse and in you all the families of the earth will be blessed" (Genesis 12:1-3).*

The key to understanding the Old Testament and God's epic within marriage is in this covenant. The curse against Satan at the fall of man and the Abrahamic Covenant are essential plots of the epic. God elects Abram to build a nation through him. There is no Israel, Jerusalem, or Ten Commandments. It is just Abram, Sarai, (Abraham and Sarah are Abram and Sarai until the end of the story when God fulfills His covenant with Abram and Sarai and changes their names) and God's covenant with Abram that He will deliver on four things. The first is land. God promises Abram a land that will be fruitful and it will be uniquely positioned so traders on land and sea will need it to reach other nations. Second, God promises to financially bless Abram and to make him into a great nation. He will use Abram's DNA and ethnicity to build a nation that will inhabit the land. Thirdly, God is going to protect his nation. Finally, God tells Abram that all the nations will be blessed through him. The nation of Abram is going to bring about the opportunity for all men to have a relationship with the one true God. Peter and Paul, who wrote in the New Testament, tell us that this was a Messianic promise:

*It is you who are the sons of the prophets and of the covenant which God made with your fathers, saying to Abram, AND IN YOUR SEED ALL THE FAMILIES OF THE EARTH SHALL BE BLESSED.*

*For you first, God raised up His Servant and sent Him to bless you by turning every one of you from your wicked ways (Acts 3:25-26).*

*There is neither Jew nor Greek, there is neither slave nor free man, there is neither male nor female; for you are all one in Christ Jesus.*

*And if you belong to Christ, then you are Abraham's descendants, heirs according to promise (Galatians 3:28-29).*

God asks only two things from Abram: "go and believe." In other words, He is saying, "Leave your home and have *faith* that I am going to provide for you what I have promised." Abram is faithful to leave and believe. However, every time Abram and Sarai struggle with belief, trouble results.

## Doubt

*Now there was a famine in the land; so Abraham went down to Egypt to sojourn there, for the famine was severe in the land. It came about when he came near to Egypt, that he said to Sarah his wife, "See now, I know that you are a beautiful woman; and when the Egyptians see you, they will say, 'This is his wife'; and they will kill me, but they will let you live.*
*"Please say that you are my sister so that it may go well with me because of you, and that I may live on account of you" (Genesis 12:10-13).*

The Bible tells us there is a famine in the land, so Abram and Sarai pack up their household and go to Egypt. Egypt had a pharaoh, so it was probably organized and prepared to feed people in the event that a famine occurred. Egypt would have been a sanctuary for many nomads like Abram and Sarai. As they are arriving in Egypt, Abram begins to worry about his life, in spite of the fact that God just said He was going to "make a nation out of him, bless those who bless him and curse those who curse him." Abram thinks someone is going to look at his sixty-five-year-old wife, think she is a babe, and want to kill him for her. Abram asks Sarai to tell a little lie. Sarai is to tell those who ask that she and Abram are sister and brother. This is a little lie because it is true, kind of. They are related, but probably just through their father. Their dad may have had multiple wives and a lot of children.

The lie backfires. Pharaoh sees Sarai, he is told she is only Abram's sister, and takes her back to the castle for himself. Like in *Indecent Proposal*, Pharaoh trades livestock good for shepherding, trading and travel, and male and female slaves to Abram for Sarai. Pharaoh's servants are now lavishing Sarai. She is being pampered and made ready for her "first night" with Pharaoh—until a plague strikes all those living in the king's house. I don't know how Pharaoh figured it out, but he quickly returns Sarai to Abram, and escorts the family and their new belongings out of town.

Obviously, Abram was not staying at a Holiday Inn Express while in Egypt. Lying to Pharaoh can't be smart. This scenario could have killed him and compromised his wife's sexual purity. God spares Abram and as He promised, God graciously uses this scenario to bless him. In Genesis chapter 13, verse 2, we read for the first time that Abram is now very rich. I think Pharaoh said, "Take your stuff and the stuff I gave you and go, so the God of Abram will spare me." However, later we are going to meet a young girl who was a part of Abram's new Egyptian acquisitions, and will be part of another bad decision that will affect this family, possibly forever.

Abram's actions are based on his doubt of God's provision. Doubt is often a part of the Christian experience. Most believers will struggle with where God is in some situation of life. The danger of doubt is when it produces an action that believes the doubt is truth. In other words, when our activities of life are motivated by doubt instead of God's Word, we will make poor choices. Those choices are sometimes called sin.

Abram made a bad decision. It is a testimony to God's great mercy that He spares Abram and blesses him.

## God Gets Specific

*Abram said, "O Lord GOD, what will You give me, since I am childless, and the heir of my house is Eliezer of Damascus?" And Abram said, "Since You have given no offspring to me, one born in my house is my heir." Then behold, the word of the LORD came to him, saying, "This man will not be your heir; but one who will come forth from your own body, he shall be your heir" (Genesis 15:2-4).*

It has been ten years since God took the initiative to tell Abram his place in the epic. Abram is beginning to think that Eliezer is going to be his heir. Eliezer is the son of a slave from Damascus, and his parents probably served on Abram's property or in his home. This was a common occurrence in the culture of Abram. If the property owner was childless, an heir was chosen from among the males already living within the household. God tells Abram that his heir is not Eliezer and reassures him that his descendant will come from his own body. God is simply telling Abram to wait on what He has promised; essentially, go and believe. *Believe that I am big enough to follow through with the promises I have made you, Abram. Believe I saved you out of Egypt, believe I gave you victory in the war of kings, believe I have provided all your possessions and believe I am capable of opening the womb of your wife.* The Bible tells us that after this conversation with God, Abram believed.

Before we go any further this may be your situation. Are you wondering what God is going to do next? While navigating the waters of patience, it important to continue with God's original plan doing the things you know He would have you to do. Abram doesn't leave the Promised Land to return home. He must be wondering what God is waiting on, but nevertheless he remains faithful to the original calling. God still doesn't give him a child, but ten years later he gives him a touch, a word of affirmation that He is still working. If this is you, begin praying for God to affirm in your life that He is still working. You may not hear an audible voice (I never have, don't know if I want to either), but you may be surprised to see how God speaks to your heart. This season will assuredly increase your epic faith as a couple.

Unfortunately, when Abram takes the news to his wife that God has confirmed they will have descendants, Sarai, seventy-five years old, must have felt the pressure of barrenness. It is a perfect scenario for the greatness of God to shine bright. Sarai, like Abram earlier, tries to accomplish God's will with what was culturally common. Sarai gives Abram her servant to sleep with him. Rationalizing that it had been ten years since God first promised He would provide an heir, "God must want us to do something." So Abram marries a slave woman, (for the sake of application I have tried to use only monogamous relationships, but unfortunately some of the key figures in the mosaic have multiple wives). He sleeps with her and they have a baby. The baby is the baby of a slave. Exactly what God said wouldn't need to happen.

## That's Gonna Leave a Mark

*So Sarai said to Abram, "Now behold, the LORD has prevented me from bearing children. Please go in to my maid; perhaps I will obtain children through her." And Abram listened to the voice of Sarai (Genesis 16:2).*

*The angel of the LORD said to her further, "Behold, you are with child, and you will bear a son; And you shall call his name Ishmael, because the LORD has given heed to your affliction.*
*"He will be a wild donkey of a man, his hand will be against everyone, and everyone's hand will be against him; and he will live to the east of all his brothers" (Genesis 16:11-12).*

Hagar and Abram have a child. He is named Ishmael. He was not conceived the way God had proclaimed to Abram, so he will not be the nation of Israel. Nevertheless, he is Abram's child and therefore will have many descendants. The Bible says God told Hagar that Ishmael would be a "wild donkey of a man, his hand will be against everyone and everyone's hand will be against him." It appears that Ishmael's descendants will be enemies to their brothers forever.

About 650 years after Christ, Mohammed claimed that the Muslim nation had descended from Ishmael. If this is true, this season of doubt and poor decisions by Abram and Sarai has created Israel's greatest enemy. Some extreme Muslim groups want genocide for the Jewish race. When we try to do the things God has called us to do in our own way, we can experience terrible consequences. There is a fine line between faithful patience and faithful action. How can we know which one we should do?

## Four Essentials

Abram and Sarai did what was acceptable in their culture, but not acceptable in God's culture. Unfortunately, our culture can be counter-God as well. It is important to realize that God does not need what is acceptable to any culture to accomplish

His will. God simply asked Abram to do two things: "go and believe." He will take care of the rest. He never asked Abram to "go and get another wife." He just wanted Abram to "go and believe." God so often just calls us to "go and believe." Not "go and get into debt," "go and lie," "go and sue," "go and cheat," "go and make it happen your way…" He simply says, "go and believe" and "I will take care of the rest." To help us with decisions of faith, I believe as Christians, God has provided tools to verify what we believe He is saying.

The first is Scripture. God does not speak against His own Word. It may sound old-fashioned or simple-minded, even foolish, but I believe that God is big enough to give me an accurate, error-free account of His Word. Scripture is reliable, and I don't have to guess which parts are true and which ones have expired, like the milk in my fridge. This reliable Holy Text tells me how much He loves me and what God expects of me. In addition to knowing Scripture, we have to follow Scripture if we expect to know God's will in certain situations. Andy Stanley said in his sermon series *Discovering God's Will*, "the more we follow God's moral will (found in the Bible) the more we will understand God's personal will."[4] God's Word is clear about sleeping with my fiancée, cheating on my taxes, murder, stealing, lying, adultery and many other things. This concept easily eliminates some culturally excepted scenarios because we know that God will not tell us to do something His Word does not confirm. Jesus made determining God's moral will simple when He said,

*AND YOU SHALL LOVE THE LORD YOUR GOD WITH ALL YOUR HEART, AND WITH ALL YOUR SOUL, AND WITH ALL YOUR MIND, AND WITH ALL YOUR STRENGTH.*

*The second is this, YOU SHALL LOVE YOUR NEIGHBOR AS YOURSELF. There is no other commandment greater than these (Mark 12:30-31).*

If an activity does not give God the glory or show a love and respect for people, there is a very good chance it is not within the parameters of God's moral will. If we will follow these two important commands, we will find that discerning God's will becomes clearer.

Secondly, we can pray and ask God to confirm what we believe He may be saying. Maybe you feel like it's time to get a house, or start a new career. Ask God to reveal His will to you through prayer. When couples come together to pray about decisions, they are making these powerful moments. Seeing God answer those prayers makes for a stronger marriage. If you struggle with praying together beyond meal times, begin to take advantage of life's opportunities to pray together. Early in our marriage, and sometimes even now, Angie and I struggle with praying about God's will for situations in our lives. But life often presents us with scenarios that require us to pray together: buying our first home, buying a car, moving to Houston, moving away from Houston, having children, loss of family members, and so on. Life will present you with opportunities to pray as a couple. Don't miss them. As a couple, begin now asking God for His will and wisdom in the big decisions of your life.

A prayerful marriage is a gift and extremely important to becoming an Epic Marriage. Couples who pray together have increased intimacy with one another. Begin taking prayer requests from one another. Pray for your future together. Maybe pray for missions, church activities and neighborhood events. Prayer connects the spiritual side each of you has. As you pray, you will find you can connect on a spiritual level you never knew was possible.

Another aspect of prayer I employ is asking God to confirm what I believe He may be calling me to do personally. I have a deep respect for my wife's ability to discern the potential dangers in a situation. I also want to have a happy wife! If I feel like God is asking my family to do something like move, give more, sacrifice more, or make a major lifestyle change, I usually pray, "God will you please give Angie the same heart you are giving me about this decision." Angie is a strong, simple believer in God. She doesn't doubt and she has a unique "spiritual gut" about God. She just knows when someone is up to no good, or if we are about to do something that is not God's best.

That brings me to a third point of discerning God's will and that is unity as a couple. Do everything within your power to maintain unity as a couple when you have to make huge decisions. God is not in the business of dividing marriages. If God is giving you a stirring to do something and your spouse does not agree, then be patient and prayerful. Ask God to change hearts, yours or your spouse's. When you seek to make unified decisions, you will make wiser decisions. You won't find yourself in a situation that is difficult with a resentful spouse to deal with because you got them into a mess. Difficult situations come with every great calling (just ask Abram and Sarai). Dealing with them as a team that made a unified prayerful decision together is much easier than going at it alone. Not only is it easier, it is God's best for you both as an epic couple.

Finally, get advice from other Christian friends or mentors. I meet with new couples all the time who move into my city and are looking for a new church home. Sometimes they love the church where I serve and stay, and sometimes they look around at what the other churches in the area are doing. When they tell me this, they usually look like they have confessed to murder. I try to reassure them that I think discovering a congregation that meets their own needs is great. My heart is not that every young married couple will come to my church. My heart is that every young married couple will surround themselves with a church family that will love and offer them wisdom or support.

These four qualities are essential to fulfilling your marriage's purpose in the epic. Living through the lens of Scripture, prayer, unity and wise counsel will lead your marriage in faith. You will find, or you may already know, that when you stray from these basic elements of faith, your marriage is not centered on God's will but your own. God's grace is good and today He wants to show you how to live out His purpose for your marriage. Go and believe His grace is enough.

## Canaan Bound

*So Sarah conceived and bore a son to Abraham in his old age, at the appointed time of which God had spoken to him. Abraham called the name of his son who was born to him, whom Sarah bore to him, Isaac (Genesis 21:2-3).*

Twenty-five years after God first spoke to Abram, God came through with His promise and His will. Abram, now ninety-nine years old, and Sarai, ninety years old, are going to be called Abraham (father of a nation) and Sarah (princess). God establishes the covenant of circumcision with Abraham and tells him that Sarah will be the "mother of a nation." God tells Abraham that he will have a child through Sarah and they will name him Isaac (literally, *he laughs)*. Andrew Peterson wrote a song about this moment in the marriage of Abraham and Sarah that depicts beautifully their realization that all God has promised them would come to fruition. Here is the lyric:

Sarah, take me by my arm
Tomorrow we are Canaan bound
Where westward sails the golden sun
And Hebron's hills are amber crowned
So bid your troubled heart be still
The grass, they say, is soft and green
The trees are tall and honey-filled
So, Sarah, come and walk with me
Like the stars across the heavens flung
Like water in the desert sprung
Like the grains of sand, our many sons
Oh, Sarah, fair and barren one
Come to Canaan, come
I trembled at the voice of God
A voice of love and thunder deep
With love He means to save us all
And Love has chosen you and me
Long after we are dead and gone
A thousand years our tale be sungHow faith compelled and bore us on
How barren Sarah bore a son
So come to Canaan, come
Where westward sails the golden sun
And Hebron's hills are amber crowned
Oh, Sarah, take me by my arm
Tomorrow we are Canaan bound[5]

I can picture this dear older couple finally finding peace at the end of a long life together, knowing they finished strong. Knowing they have fulfilled what they believe to be God's will for their lives, they can pass away to Canaan in peace. They will rest securely placed within the epic of Christ.

In the Bible, there is a book called Romans. It reveals many profound truths of faith. It says:

*...if you confess with your mouth that Jesus is Lord and believe in your heart that God raised Him from the dead, you will be saved; for with the heart a person believes, resulting in righteousness, with the mouth he confesses, resulting in salvation (Romans 10:9-10).*

A relationship with Jesus is a modern Canaan; it begins with an honest prayer confessing you are not perfect and have failed God by not living for His glory. In addition, you believe in your heart that God sent His son to die for your inability to live a sinless life in order that we be restored to a right relationship with Him. When you do these things, you will be in right relationship with the Creator of the universe. So if you haven't yet, believe in your heart that Christ is true and ask God to forgive your failures, to be the King of your life, and commit to serve and acknowledge His glory all the days of your life. You don't have to be perfect to pray this prayer and you will fail after you pray this prayer. I know this because I fail daily! This relationship is not dependent on our perfection. It is dependent on His perfect grace. God's grace is unlike anything you have ever experienced on earth!

Once you make this extremely serious commitment to God, you must tell someone. There is a spiritual adversary who wants to disrupt your relationship with God and will by all means try to move your heart away from Him towards the things of this world. Get involved in a local church that believes the Bible is perfect truth and all you need is God's grace to be forgiven from sins. Surround your family with others who believe like you. It will help you defend yourself from the devil and join the multitudes who believe in God to penetrate a dark and desperate world with the amazing message of Christ's epic. If you already have a relationship with Jesus Christ but have dropped out of the journey, I want to encourage you to rekindle your relationship with Him. His grace is waiting.

Faith will be an essential element to your journey in having an Epic Marriage. Later we will discover that making decisions that reflect the love and passion of Christ for His church will be difficult. A faith in Jesus Christ as Lord of you life is essential. Professing Jesus as Lord of your life is no small matter. It is a major decision that requires a death of self in order for your life to give glory to God. Later we will consider more of what this means. In order for your marriage to fulfill its purposes, it is essential that both of you have surrendered to Jesus Christ as Lord and Savior of your life. Simply pray together; *"Lord we confess that we have not been living the way You have desired for us to live; please forgive us for our sins. Today we profess that You are Lord and Savior of our lives and we commit to living for You for the rest of our lives. Thank you for dying on the cross for our sins and restoring us into a right relationship with God. Give us strength for the rest of our Journey with You, amen. "* All it takes to have a relationship with Jesus Christ and to begin your Epic Marriage is professing your need for God and His leadership over your life.

Secondly, you will need to have epic faith in God's Word. The Bible as we know it is God's Word to us. Some have referred to it as a love letter to humanity. In the end Christians believe that the Bible speaks for God and He knows what is best for us. As our culture changes, some have tried to change the meaning of Scripture. However, I believe that God's Word is still a perfect revelation of salvation and of ways He desires for us to live. As we begin this epic, just relax. Try not to bring your culture, personal preferences and prejudices into God's word for you. Pretend for a while that He knows what is best for you and our culture does not.

What are you hearing from God as a couple or as an individual? Maybe you have taken a few missteps by taking things into your own hands. It's okay. God was faithful to forgive and use Abraham and Sarah to accomplish a glorious beginning to His Son's legacy. God is faithful to forgive and use you as well. As you learn to live to reveal Christ to the world, hold tightly to each other, God's Word, prayer and wise counsel. God will lead you right where He wants you in His epic. Now go and believe He has a special purpose for your marriage. Add a new dimension of faith to your marriage as you grow and discover God's will for your lives together.

Faith is a funny thing. My wife is the one who has the most faith in the family. I question and doubt everything. It is just who I am. I have always been a critic, while my wife simply trusts her Heavenly Father in all things. Her style of faith is inspiring and epic. If you find you are more like me and your faith is more critical, I want to encourage you to never stop wrestling with what you know to be true. When I first became a Christian there were two things I just had to accept in faith and the rest was up for debate. First, there is a God who sent His Son Jesus to die for my sins. In addition to saving us, God did not leave us stranded, but left us the Holy Spirit and the Holy Scriptures. So, I must trust the Scriptures to be wholly and completely true in matters of salvation. As I doubt, wonder, and deal with subjects of faith, I am sure to hold on to my two anchors of God and Scripture. In the end, my doubts have become convictions that shape the person I am today. I hope you will join me in the daily struggle for an epic faith.

## Discussion Questions with Your Spouse or Small Group

*What is something you feel like God is calling you to do/ have?*

*Have you ever seen God work through a situation that could have been tragic?*

*How can we know that we are allowing God to be God when we pursue the desires He has given us?*

# Chapter 4
# Dealing with Baggage:
# Isaac and Rebekah

## More Caught Than Taught

What have you learned from your parents? Have you ever sat down and thought about the personality traits, habits and skills you may have learned from them? When Angie and I counsel a newlywed or nearlywed couple, the question of parental modeling always comes up. It turns out that parents have a major influence in the way their children live as adults. Studies report that children begin modeling their parents' behavior before one year of age. My son Austin is thirteen months old. Angie and I have made it a habit to sign to him "I love you" when we leave him to go to work or run errands. He recently started signing back that he loves us. He doesn't know what it means, but he knows this is what the people who love him do when they leave. Austin is already modeling his parents.

In a government study on the research regarding the prediction of adolescent risky behaviors, it was reported, "family related variables play in the prediction of various adolescent risky behaviors."[6] These areas of risk include promiscuous sexual behavior, marijuana use, alcoholism, delinquency and poor social skills. The most disruptive family environment for a child to grow up in is a divorced family. Divorced parents are twice as likely to have children who engage in risky activities. There are also indicators that these risky behaviors carry over into adulthood. Thus, if a child grows up in a divorced family he or she is likely to have a divorce when they are adults.

What have you learned from your parents? Most of what you have learned from them was never said or taught—it was caught. You saw them do it or they accepted what you did and you learned at a very young age that certain behaviors were acceptable and some were not. How did your parents fight? Did they fight at all? *Parents* magazine reports, "helping your child learn how to control her temper begins with your behavior. You're the role model."[7] We learn from our parents to yell when we are angry, to dodge responsibility when it is our fault, or to cry our way out of hurtful situations. How about sex? Can't imagine it? I can't blame you. Your parents did it, and hopefully they still do it. What you learned from them in regards to sex is taking its positive or negative toll on your marriage. Work ethic, generosity, religion, God, handling money, alcohol use, pornography—all of these traits, habits, truths and addictions can be learned from our parents.

You may be like me. I grew up with divorced parents and very little God in my life yet, when the opportunity came to respond to God's call on my life to follow Him, I answered yes. Nobody raised me to be a Christian. I was a teenager in need of answers and I found them in the one Yahweh God. I professed Christ to be my Lord and Savior and asked Him to lead my life. After I became Christian, I began the shaping process of becoming like Christ and that process chiseled out many of the risky behaviors I picked up in adolescence. I am not by any means done, but I can now look back on my life and see what I learned as a young boy from my parents and what I need to do now as a Christian man is not always the same thing. What have you learned from your parents?

## Isaac's Family Life

*God visited Sarah exactly as he said he would; God did to Sarah what he promised: Sarah became pregnant and gave Abraham a son in his old age, and at the very time God had set. Abraham named him Isaac. When his son was eight days old, Abraham circumcised him just as God had commanded...*

*The baby grew and was weaned. Abraham threw a big party on the day Isaac was weaned (Genesis 21:1-4 and 8 [The Message]).*

Just as God promised, Isaac was born to Abraham and Sarah. Because of the covenant God made with Abraham, Isaac had an incredible future ahead of Him. He was going to receive the blessings his father was promised and continue the lineage of Israel. Even with all the blessings of the Abrahamic Covenant, Isaac would still deal with behavior he learned from his parents.

Three key events happened in the life of Isaac. The first is the banishing of his half-brother Ishmael. Ishmael was born of a mistake Abraham and Sarah made when they tried to rush God's timing. They had been promised a child and yet were without one for so long they agreed to have a child through the Egyptian servant Hagar. Hagar and Sarah become enemies from this point forward. However, Hagar and her son Ishmael still lived with Abraham and Sarah. When Isaac was weaned, Ishmael taunted his younger brother. This event sent Sarah into a raging fit and she commanded Abraham to throw Hagar and

Ishmael out of the house. Abraham did it and Hagar and Ishmael went to begin quite possibly the Muslim nation. This event was crucial to Isaac's understanding of God's timing. Isaac saw first-hand and probably heard during his entire upbringing not to force God's will and to wait for His perfect timing. If God promises, He will deliver.

The second major event of Isaac's upbringing is his near-death experience at the hand of his father. God had commanded Abraham to sacrifice Isaac. Can you imagine such a request? As I read this text, I thought to myself, I would really need to hear a voice from God to be obedient to this. If you grew up in church, you know the story and so it doesn't surprise you that God provided a sacrifice in the end. But if you are reading this passage in Genesis for the first time you must be thinking, *Is God crazy? Why would He give Abraham a son and then ask him to sacrifice him?* I am sure this was Abraham's thought: *It took twenty-five years to get him and now you want me to give him back!*

Isaac, by the way, is asking questions as well, "Dad, where is the sacrifice? We are at the altar, but where is the sacrifice?" Abraham answers his son with epic faith that God will provide an alternative. Finally, at the last possible moment, God provides a ram in the thicket and tells Abraham that he does not need to sacrifice his one and only son. In Abraham's final days, he lives trusting that God would provide for him even in the worst of circumstances.

The third major event in the upbringing of Isaac is the loss of his mom. We really don't hear a lot about how Isaac deals with this loss, but we learn from passages to come that her loss is going to have a profound impact on his emotions. God will use a wonderful, servant-hearted young woman to meet this need Isaac has for being comforted.

## Love at First Sight

On his deathbed, Abraham sends out a trusted servant to Mesopotamia (Abraham's homeland) to find a wife for Isaac. The servant may have traveled many days from Canaan to Mesopotamia. The Scripture says he was the oldest servant in the household, so he may have been married; either way, he now has to find a wife for another man. While traveling he must have wondered, *What makes a great wife?* Over and over again in his head he could have been thinking, *What would I want in a wife?* It is interesting he did not choose things like beauty, pedigree (great parents), tall, short, skinny, athletic. He had one characteristic in mind.

When the servant finally arrives in Mesopotamia, he stops at a spring where daughters come to get water for their families. The servant spots a beautiful young woman. She must have been graceful and tan with long dark hair and an expression of purity and innocence. Yet she has not passed the test. Finally, the young girl offers the servant some water. He accepts, and then she goes the next step and offers to water his camels. She passed! "What makes a great wife?" said the servant. "A servant-hearted wife." It was natural for her to offer to do more than what was expected. She was graceful, hospitable and friendly. This was the woman for Isaac. The servant goes through all the formalities with the family and he and the woman begin the journey back to Canaan to meet her future husband.

We fast-forward to find Isaac has just returned from a long journey and he is meditating in a field. It may have been sunset in the green valley of Negev. Plush land surrounds him as he wonders on the things of God and what He has shown him over his lifetime. During this time of meditation, he looks up to see camels, so he begins to walk towards them.

Rebekah sees a fair and handsome man from the distance and asks, "Who is he?" She must have been hoping it was Isaac, her future husband.

The servant answers, "That is my master."

Quickly Rebekah veils herself because she is a woman of purity and honor. Scripture carries the reader along this love-at-first sight scene so quickly that in a matter of six verses this couple meets and gets married. It was through marriage that Isaac finally finds comfort from the loss of his mother. God uses this passionate young couple to reveal the next scene in His epic. Their marriage is sweet and comforting, but it has a greater purpose in God's epic will.

## Risky Marriage

Like every marriage, Isaac and Rebekah's will come with some baggage. Isaac is given two opportunities to repeat the mistakes of his parents. The first comes in the form of bearing children. Scripture tells us that Rebekah was barren. Isaac and Rebekah have a choice early on in marriage to do what Isaac's parents did. Isaac had his choice of maidservants and this would have been an acceptable practice in their culture. However, Isaac remembers something about his half-brother. Maybe Sarah offered her opinion on Hagar and the whole situation, or Abraham gave Isaac wisdom one day when he shared with him about the "birds and bees." Isaac prays on behalf of his wife. Oh if only more men would pray on behalf of their wives! Pray not to change them, but to bless them.

*Isaac prayed hard to God for his wife because she was barren. God answered his prayer and Rebekah became pregnant (Genesis 25:21).*

What is your situation? God's epic proposed Isaac to have children. Isaac's children were part of God's sovereign plan for humanity. All of us have a purpose in God's epic of revealing Christ to the world, and all of us have something we are bringing into marriage that may interfere with our purpose as a couple. God may be calling you to be great givers, yet you have learned nothing of money except to keep it for yourself. God may be calling you to not have kids so you can focus on another ministry He is preparing for you. God may be calling you to have a healthy marriage as a witness to other couples in your neighborhood, but you find yourself in front of the television every night. What has God stirred your heart to do for His glory?

For God's glory, Isaac was going to have children with Rebekah. What about you? My hope is that you will recognize your purpose as a couple and consider how your upbringing may be hindering or promoting it. I think God calls us to do things that we are not always parentally groomed for or good at. I think He does this for two reasons. First, He gets more glory. Second, you grow to be more like His Son, Jesus Christ. God wants to use you and make you holy. Pursue Him and He will do both in you.

Isaac is presented with a second opportunity to deal with the baggage of his upbringing. In fact, the parallel with his parents is eerie. This part of Isaac and Rebekah's story begins with, "Now there was a famine in the land…" This time instead of going to Egypt as his parents did, God tells Isaac to stay put, and He will bless him and make his descendants great. Isaac obeys

God. He, Rebekah and their twins stay in Gerar. Nevertheless, trouble finds Isaac. The men of Gerar notice Rebekah and begin to ask about her. When Isaac is asked if he is married to her, he fearfully says, "She is my sister." Isaac, like his father, lies due to fear and doubt. The baggage of his parents follows him right into marriage. Isaac's family is living in the land of the Philistines. The king of the Philistines catches Isaac romantically caressing Rebekah and calls him on his bluff. The king orders that no men are to touch Rebekah and scolds Isaac for lying because someone could have slept with his wife.

The baggage that Isaac never dealt with was fear and doubt. Like his father before him, Isaac could have been killed for this unnecessary lie, but God not only spares him, He blesses him. A strong lesson every couple can take from this story is not to make decisions based on fear. Make decisions based on promise. God has promised many things to those who follow Jesus Christ. The most important is that He has a plan for your life and will use life's experiences to shape you and make you holy.

## What Have You Learned from Your Parents?

Epic couples deal with what they bring to their marriage from their families. You may have had wonderful godly parents who reared you in an environment that has allowed you to thrive as a person with no crutches. You are rare. I hope you will strive to pass on the godly legacy that they passed to you. For the rest of us, we have some baggage that we need to consider. Marriage surfaces all kinds of issues that lurk at the bottom of our souls—selfishness, addictions, critical thoughts, pessimism, commitment issues and the list goes on and on. What has surfaced in your life? Don't accept it, strive to live past it. God has allowed you to realize this trait so you can begin the process of growing out of it and not passing it onto your kids. It is a promise from God that by His grace and through your willingness, you can break a cycle of sin. You may find the cycle you need to break is the very purpose God has called you to.

My little sister and I have watched up to six divorces in our immediately family between our parents, multiple stepparents and grandparents. Divorce is a rampant cancer in my family, and it did nothing but hurt everyone involved. The sting of my parents' divorce is still felt today almost thirty years later. My passion, purpose, and the cycle I am passionate about breaking is divorce. The common denominators I saw in all the divorces were bad communication habits, selfish motivators, and a lack of a commitment to Jesus Christ as Lord. I have strived in my marriage to be selfless, communicate even the worst information, and stay committed to Jesus Christ. Luckily (if you believe in that sort of thing), Angie is committed to working just as hard as me. So when I drop the ball she is there to hold us together and vice versa. This passion has leaked out of my marriage into my ministry. The reason for this book and the hope of my life is that I will be part of God's epic by restoring and strengthening marriages so that Christ is revealed through these holy relationships.

What passionate pursuit has God called you to break free from? Maybe you already have. How is this passion going to leak out of your home and positively affect the lives of others? As you deal with the baggage of your family these are questions you must ask yourself. All throughout Scripture, God uses obedient people to do marvelous works. Be obedient to His Word and His will for your life. Trust in His promises and begin to experience the freedom that comes from making wise decisions regarding your past.

As a couple the most important task of dealing with baggage is communication. The steps that follow communication are dependent upon your personal situation. Be sure you make an effort to have an honest discussion with one another about the areas of life and marriage that have been poorly modeled for you. As you begin to discuss and pray together concerning the baggage of your marriage, you will find peace. As you heal and discover the way out of the darkness, a deep desire will be birthed in you to help others regarding these very issues. This is part of your epic purpose. Receiving God's grace, learning from the mistakes of your parents, and helping others the way you have been helped.

You are also a child of promise as Isaac was. As children of God and followers of Christ, we are promised to be set free from the chains that bind. You don't have to live with your baggage any longer. Throw it out and reveal the power of God's epic.

## Discussion Questions with Your Spouse or Small Group

*What have you learned from your parents? How has it affected your marriage positively or negatively?*

*Why is it important to find comfort in your spouse? How can your spouse do a better job of comforting you? How can you do better job comforting your spouse?*

*What keeps prayer out of your marriage?*

*What can you do better to pray for each other and pray together?*

*Regarding your baggage, what do you think is your purpose in God's epic?*

# Chapter 5
# A Protective Wife:
# Moses and Zipporah

## A Growing Family

The legacy of Abraham continues through Isaac. Isaac and Rebekah have Jacob and Esau. Jacob adds twelve sons to the family of Israel. Jacob's sons become the twelve tribes of Israel and they have many children. Joseph, one of Jacob's sons, becomes very influential in Egypt. During a famine, the family of Israel once again needs relief. They find it through Joseph's position in Egypt. As the second in command to Pharaoh, Joseph is able to provide a new home and food for the struggling family. All of the family of Israel moves to Goshen, Egypt, and settle there to grow under the authority, care, and protection of the Egyptians.

Decades pass and Egypt gets a new Pharaoh not familiar with Joseph. The new Pharaoh recognizes the family of Israel has grown larger than Egypt. Out of fear that Israel may one day rise up and take over Egypt, Pharaoh puts Israel under the bonds of slavery to build storehouses. Some scholars say it was during this period that the great pyramids of Egypt were built.

To help control the growing strength and population of Israel, Pharaoh orders all male Israelites to be killed at birth. However, by God's protection many sons were still being born in Israel. One mother hid her special son for three months. When she decided she could hide him no longer, she placed him in a basket so he could possibly float down the Nile River to safety. He did just that. The daughter of Pharaoh saved Moses from the waters of the Nile. She named him Moses and then unknowingly recruited his mother to nurse and care for him until he was weaned.

Moses grows up under the privileged care of Pharaoh's house. Then one day he killed an Egyptian guard when his heart was burdened by the treatment the Israelites were receiving under Egyptian slavery. After this, Moses was forced to pack his things and run to the wilderness of the Middle East for fear that Pharaoh might kill him for what he had done.

It was in this wilderness that Moses finds a wife and begins a family. Moses' wife is one of the seven daughters of a priest in Midian. Moses meets her when he saves the priest's seven daughters from harassment by some Egyptian men. After living many years with the priest of Midian, he gives his daughter, Zipporah, to Moses to be his wife. They begin a family and a life in Midian. Around this time, the Egyptians begin to treat the family of Israel worse and Israel cries out to God. God hears their cries and calls on Moses to help.

Most of us are familiar with the story of the burning bush and Moses. While Moses is shepherding in the wilderness, he sees a bush burning. This bush is odd because it never burns up. When I read this passage of Scripture, I can't help but to think of the burning bush scene of the epic movie, *The Ten Commandments*. If you have not seen it, the scene looks like someone took a red highlighter and colored in the camera that filmed a bush. It worked. It never burns up and it is not quite Spielberg material, but worth renting. As Moses approaches, from the bush God tells him to remove his sandals for he is on holy ground. It is here that God calls Moses to set free the family of Israel from their captivity in Egypt. Moses reluctantly accepts his calling and packs up his wife and kids to make their journey to Egypt.

As Moses, Zipporah and the kids are traveling, something very strange happens. This event has stumped and confused scholars for years. I don't hope to shed new light on the event with the exception of highlighting the importance of marriage in God's epic. Moses was not called to have kids, add to the tribes of Israel, or even get married. Moses had one epic calling and one epic purpose and it was a passion of his heart from the time that he was a young man. He had always wanted to see Israel free. Now God has called on him to do it. God will use Moses' marriage in a unique way to help him achieve his epic purpose thus, creating an Epic Marriage.

## A Protective Wife

*Now it came about at the lodging place on the way that the LORD met him and sought to put him to death.*

*Then Zipporah took a flint and cut off her son's foreskin and threw it at Moses' feet, and she said, "You are indeed a bridegroom of blood to me."*

*So He let him alone. At that time she said, "You are a bridegroom of blood"—because of the circumcision.*

While Moses and the family are traveling, Scripture says God threatens the life of Moses. The reader can't tell how God threatens Moses' life. It could be a Darth Vader thing like in *Star Wars*. While using the force, Vader holds up the Imperial commander by the neck. But that's not God's style. God is bigger than the obvious. I think Moses got sick. It was not uncommon for the Israelites of this day to attribute everything to God's will and power. A common expression was, "If God wills it." Is it going to rain? "If God wills it." Will we settle in Canaan? "If God wills it." Zipporah and the original readers would consider sickness to be God's will and possibly His way of getting Moses' attention. The sickness would cause Moses to be so weak he could not attend to himself and this would have stopped the caravan to Egypt.

Zipporah is acutely aware of what is happening and somehow senses that God is disciplining Moses for something he had done wrong. There are no Ten Commandments yet, no book of Deuteronomy or Leviticus to reveal appropriate custom laws. All Moses and Zipporah would have known was God commanded Abraham to circumcise Isaac to institute a covenant of circumcision for generations to come. Circumcision became the sign of a covenant relationship between the descendants of Abraham and God. It appears that Moses missed this step with his children. Before God allows Moses to fulfill his epic purpose, he must get his relationship with his Creator right.

Scripture wastes no time between these two scenes. Abraham is struck with a deadly illness and Zipporah immediately responds. She takes a rough, jagged piece of flint and quickly circumcises her son. Ouch! There is no other way to imagine it. Ouch! Why not go to the priest with a flint that may have been more precise and less painful? Why did God cause this to happen in the wilderness? It is all very suspicious. One truth stands out to me. God is extremely concerned about our relationship with Him.

Sin separates us from God. Moses had one sin counted against him and that was the failure to place his sons under the covenant of Abraham. In the Old Testament and now, God has a special communion with His followers. Thankfully, no one has to be circumcised after Jesus died on the cross for our redemption. However, sin can still distance us from God. When we fail to do what God has commanded us to do in Scripture, we fall short of God's best for His glory and our lives resulting in sin.

If you are living in a habitual condition that is contrary to what the Bible says about living, God is trying to get your attention. Cut off the sin and restore your rich deep relationship with God. You may need to cut off the sin to begin an incredible relational journey with God. Your marriage will never be epic until sin is both recognized and dealt with. God's grace is sufficient for you to begin this process of overcoming whatever habit you have that is not God's best. We all have them. Expose it to the Light and the darkness of sin will fade. Its appeal will no longer blind you and suddenly you will find freedom and peace.

After Zipporah circumcises her son, she touches the foot of Moses with the bloody foreskin and says, "You are indeed a bridegroom of blood to me." She says this twice, once before Moses is healed, and another time after he was healed. There are many reasons she could have said this. Scholars have not expressed a unified position on what Zipporah's words may have meant. Here is what I perceive. A bridegroom is a marriage partner. A bridegroom of blood is a marriage partner with blood involved. The Bible says that she said this because of the circumcision. Therefore, the blood involved must be the blood of the child and the bridegroom is her marriage with Moses. A simple solution may be that she circumcised her son as the bridegroom of Moses. Through marriage, she had taken on the role of her husband for a brief period of time in order to make things right between her husband and God. She could have said, "Because I am your wife, and you are my husband, we are one. I am circumcising our son so you will be spared the penalty you are facing for failing to do this."

Scholars may continue to debate what is meant by the words of Zipporah, but there is one thing that is very clear. Zipporah was there for her husband when he needed her most. She could have left him there in the desert to die. She could have bombarded him with nagging about his inadequacy as a role model for his children. She could have done anything else, but she chose to step into a spiritual mess to help clean it up. Zipporah is an epic wife. She understands the importance of her family's epic calling and her husband's role in God's plan. If a marriage is going to be epic, a wife must at times be willing to step into the role of a spiritual mediator. She does this by interceding and practicing the things of God in order to hopefully one day save her husband from the fruits of failure.

## A Serving Wife

I never met a wife who didn't want the best for her husband. I never met a woman who didn't want to see her husband grow spiritually. It is very possible and highly likely that if you are reading this book, you already have the heart of an epic wife. You want God's very best for your husband, you want to see God's will worked out through your husband and you would even shed some blood to see it happen. However, many wives want to be epic, but they don't know the first step to take. As a male, a husband, and a father I would like to share with you how you can be an epic wife. I have no credentials, no Ph.D., and no expert survey; just years of experience as a husband and as a pastor to young married adults.

There are three main components to every human. They are the emotional, physical and the spiritual components of humanity. Music, entertainment, experience, and religion all appeal to these aspects of our being. Men function within these three levels on a daily basis. So it makes sense that God would design marriage to complement and support these areas as we seek His glory. I believe a wife and a husband are to meet the needs of each other in these three areas. It is our duty as couples to support one another in the emotional, physical and spiritual realms. However, as I said earlier, if a partner fails at meeting needs it first is our duty to reveal Christ. Needs in marriage not being met are no excuse for a divorce or bitterness. I believe that if we are truly seeking to make God the center of our lives and Christ the reflection of our marriage, the needs we have will be met. You will discover them and it will become a joy for each of you to do this for one another. In the meantime, here are some suggested practices.

## Protecting the Spiritual

Zipporah clearly stepped up in two areas when she saved Moses. To circumcise her son was a spiritual act. Circumcision was a covenant established by God to represent the covenant He had with Abraham. The closest modern equivalent of this would be a father handing over his daughter's hand in a marriage ceremony. The father as the head of the household typically does this. So when it came to circumcision it was highly unusual for Mom to do it. Moses' life was on the line, so Zipporah had to step into an unnatural role considering her usual role in the family.

How can a wife protect her husband spiritually? It begins with prayer. Prayer is the most powerful tool you have for spiritually protecting your husband. Prayer begins with a relationship with Jesus Christ. Don't try praying for your husband without first surrendering your life to the Lordship of Christ. As you begin a relationship with Jesus and continue your journey, God will give you powerful insight in how and what to pray for your husband. God knows the deeper issues and the purpose He has for your husband. With His guidance, you will find yourself praying the most effective prayers for him.

In order for Zipporah to know how to help her husband she had to know what it was God wanted from him. You will never know how to effectively pray for your husband unless you have an ongoing relationship with God. Begin praying Scripture over your husband's life. The proverbs are full of practical and powerful prayer material. Read them and other books in the Bible and seek to become a scholar on the nature of God. Pray that God will reveal His nature to you so that you will know how to better pray for your husband.

As you progress in your prayer life and in your relationship with your husband, begin asking him for prayer requests. Ask your husband how you can pray for him. He probably has not been asked this in months or worse, years! He will be shocked and honored to know that you're praying for him all day. You will be amazed to see how he changes and grows because of this simple daily question, "Honey, how can I pray for you?"

Another way you can support your husband spiritually is encouraging his spiritual leadership. Ask him to pray for you, to pray with the kids and to pray before meals. Ask him to read Scripture with you at night. Angie and I go through seasons of having nightly times together reading God's Word. Lately, I have been reading a John Piper devotional before bed and I will share with her some simple truths that I have gained from it right before we turn out the lights. In the past (before kids!) we used to have a lot more fun with our nightly devotional time. Use your marital imagination. You don't have to make this time stuffy. Make it an experience, make it enjoyable, and do it as a team.

## Protecting the Physical

Zipporah physically protects her husband by saving his life. If she had not acted fast, risked getting bloody causing her son immense pain, and performed the act she may have never even seen done before, Moses would have died. There were many factors to overcome, but the life of her husband was worth it. I hope that you will never have to be in a position like Zipporah's. In the meantime, what can you do to protect your husband physically?

The physical area under the most attack for men is in the realm of sex. Men are a visually stimulated gender. American men live in one of the most sexually driven visual cultures in the world. Billboards, television shows, internet, magazines, and even social functions bombard men with exhausting images of other women. Exhausting? Yes exhausting. Men are exhausted by these images because it is a man's responsibility to guard his eyes. An old book of wisdom in the Bible is the book of Job. It is about a man undergoing extreme devastation is his business, health and family life. The Bible calls Job a good and upright man. Job wonders why God has allowed these terrible things to befall on him. One of the things Job attributes to his uprightness is a covenant he has made with his eyes. "I have made a covenant with my eyes; How then could I gaze at a virgin?" (Job 31:1).

Like Job, men need to make a covenant with their eyes committing that they will not look at another woman the way they look at their wife. If not, a wife's attempts to protect her husband physically will be futile. A husband may be thinking, "If she starts helping me first, then maybe I can make this covenant." For some reason it does not work that way. You must first choose to make a covenant with your eyes, praise God for His forgiveness, and then begin to have a new outlook on your world. When you look at a woman lustfully, you are being greedy and you are mentally telling God that what He has provided is not good enough. There is no room in marriage or Christianity for this. A man's mindset must change so he can look at women with love and respect not greed and lust.

In addition, a man should seek out an older, merciful, and trusted friend and ask him to pray for you to help you keep your new covenant. The decision to expose this sin to light by sharing it with a friend will quickly dissolve the darkness of lust. Don't worry about judgment or condemnation from your peers. It is only by God's grace this journey is possible to begin and possible to continue. For some men this will be a very difficult step requiring a lot of God's grace. Remember, His grace is sufficient, He will see you through this commitment.

If a woman is married to a man willing to fight for his purity, she can help. A wife must first understand that her husband really has greater physical needs than she does. There are exceptions, but they are not the rule. Men typically need more sex than women do. There is an actual physiological pressure involved in a man's need for intimacy. You can protect your husband first with communication. How often does your husband need to make love? Everyone is different, but what I usually tell couples looking for a "normal" frequency of physical intimacy is, "minimally, once a week for him, once a month for her." Have an honest discussion with your husband about how often he needs to make love. There are boundaries.

Don't ever feel pressured to make love every day and remember it takes two for intimacy. This is not a one-sided deal. He has a responsibility to meet your intimacy needs as well.

How often should you commit as a couple to make love? In 2004, *Marriage Partnership Magazine* surveyed Christian married couples about their sex lives. It revealed that 73% of married couples made love as much as twice a week or at least once a month, 5% made love daily, and 14% either practically never had sex or only did once a year.[8] I think the 5% mentioned are newlyweds and the 14% that never make love have major marital problems. Try for the average of once a week. If both of you are happy making love every other week or twice a week that is fine too. Just find a sexual rhythm that fits you as a couple.

Another word for the husbands—making love is a glorious thing that should be mutually enjoyed by both of you. Husbands can become so focused on their pleasure that they neglect to sexually satisfy their wife. This is not because you don't want to. I believe every man has an inner James Bond! Of course, you want to satisfy your wife, but you may not know how. The movies never get it right and the locker-room is no place to discuss such a personal matter. Communication is paramount for providing for your wife's sexual needs. She is not turned on sexually the same way you are and so this makes it difficult to know what exactly puts her in the right frame of mind to have an orgasm. Wait a few hours or even until the next day and ask your wife what worked for her and what didn't while you were making love. Don't be embarrassed if she is surprisingly blunt and don't be hesitant to drag it out of her if she is overly shy about the subject. The last thing she wants to do is hurt your feelings. This is an important conversation to have and it will lead to a healthier marriage in the end. Remember, 58% of couples who talk about sex once a month say they are "very satisfied" with their marriage.[9] Go ahead and talk about it!

An epic wife protects her husband physically with honest communication and action concerning the real intimate physical needs her husband has. When couples are willing to talk about their sex life together, they not only support an Epic Marriage, but they will also have and epic sex life.

## Protecting the Emotional

You may be saying to yourself right now, "Protecting the emotional? But my husband is not emotional." Let me assure you he is. Not only is he emotional, but you are the most powerful force in your husbands emotional life. Something happens to a man in marriage that does not happen in any other arena of his life. A man gives his heart to his wife. He promises to love her, care for her, be with her until the end and he shares with her his secrets and feelings. Even the slightest bit of sharing from a man is letting his wife into the chambers of his heart that no one has ever ventured. With this privilege comes great joy and great responsibility.

Zipporah's actions on the way to Egypt did not give us a good example of how to protect the emotions of a husband. She did save his life so I am sure that made Moses very happy! Concerning his protection in this realm of his life, it is important that an epic wife respect her husband. Respect is something your husband craves more than anything. It is the reason men pursue wealth, possessions, connections, and positions. Men deeply desire respect from others. Respect is also essential to a man's sexual fulfillment. Men have reported that if their wife were to make endless love to them simply out of duty and accommodation versus love and respect that they would still not be sexually satisfied.[10]

Shanti Feldhahn in her book, *For Women Only,* reveals seven essential truths every woman should know about her man. Her first point and probably most important point is men need respect from their wives. She reports that 80% of men say most of their conflicts are due to feeling disrespected.[11] She later encourages wives to have unconditional respect. Unconditional respect is not dependent on a man's actions. It is a core belief of a woman to respect her husband no matter what. This may be counter to how you think things should work. Most women think their husbands should first be good so he can "earn" my respect. Shanti says no. If you first respect him, he will raise to level at which he feels respected. This comes down to an inner resolve in your heart that commits to respecting him because you believe this how God would want you to treat him (as he should you, don't worry his is coming!).

Shanti gives five areas where women can show and need to show respect to their husbands. The first is in the area of decision-making. There is a time and a way to question your husband's judgment. Shanti warns women not to be caught up in proving she is more efficient, effective or right.[12] Instead, embrace the decisions your husband makes and at the same time place your decisions on the table as viable options. It's all in how you do it, not in a yelling and badgering way. Be graceful like the woman he first fell in love with. I promise you will see an immediate change in his confidence and in the way he treats you.

Respect his abilities.[13] Men love this! How many times have you been talking to your husband about a situation or problem and he, without an invitation, mind you, offers his advice? Men love to show their abilities. Respect him by asking for help. You might say, "I do, but he still complains when he has to pull himself from ESPN to help."

To that I would ask, "How did you ask for help?" Think about your tone and your choice of words. Even your past requests will affect a man's feeling of respect when you ask him to help you. Try using a loving tone, with gently crafted words to get his assistance. It is the same way you would want him to treat you.

Shanti's third and fourth suggestions are important, but mostly self-explanatory. She suggests that you respect a man's communication and respect him in public. To this insight, I would only like to add that respecting your husband publicly and privately is essential to protecting his emotions. If you, the woman he loves are not safe then who is? Be a sanctuary to your husband. Hold to yourself the secrets and the hurts your husband may be dealing with. There is no appropriate platform for any spouse to disrespect their partner.

Finally, Shanti encourages women to respect their husbands in their assumptions.[14] Assume the best of your husband. Satan wants to tempt you to assume the worse. He fills your heart and mind with the negative emotions that feed anger and bitterness. Anger and bitterness have no place in an Epic Marriage. Assume your husband has the best intentions in all his actions. They may be wrong and need to be addressed, but not from a negative view.

For example, if your husband is constantly coming home late from work and missing out on family time, that's a problem. Don't assume he hates his family and would rather be at work than home. Instead, it is more likely he is feeling pressure to be at work by the boss or because of the bills at home he has to pay. Maybe there is a problem at home. Trust me, he would rather be with a happy you than in some asbestos-roofed office working for a boss who would not miss him if he were gone. Again, communication is essential. Not nagging communication, positive communication will protect your husband's emotional life.

## A Modern Day Zipporah

Protecting your husband's life is one of your purposes and roles in an Epic Marriage. Like Zipporah, protecting your husband will at times be difficult, but the result of praying for him, making epic love to him and respecting him will make for an amazing marriage. An Epic Marriage will bring the most glory to God. In the next chapter, I will talk mostly to the husbands and their role in an Epic Marriage. It is important to note that if you are a husband married to a woman unwilling to be your modern day Zipporah that is no excuse for you to give up on the marriage. Your desire for protection in the spiritual, sexual and emotional realms is real and legitimate. However, her failure to do these things is not a just cause for divorce. Epics are great stories that require tough times. Cling to God and endure this time. Be her sanctuary and pray for her daily. Don't give up hope in what the God of all glory and creation can accomplish in your bride.

I highly recommend that all epic wives pick up a copy of Shanti Feldhahn's book *For Women Only.* It is a powerful married life-changing book. I recently used it in a couples' Bible study. After we finished the book, many of the husbands came to me afterwards and said essentially the same thing, "That was everything I have ever wanted my wife to know about me, but I never knew how to tell her." Becoming an epic wife takes practice, grace and time. Begin the journey now and allow God's grace to be your fuel. Be epic for His glory and He will bless you every time.

## The Epic Marriage Continues

The epic of Christ continues through the marriage of Moses and Zipporah. Because Zipporah was a protective wife, Moses' life was spared. Moses and his family arrive in Egypt and by the power of God he set the family of Israel free from the bondage of Egypt. Moses and Zipporah will shepherd Israel through the wilderness for the rest of their lives. God delivers the Ten Commandment to Moses and uses him to lead the family of Israel to their promised land of Canaan. Israel is now over a million strong. A disciple of Moses, Joshua, will lead Israel to take the land of Canaan from the Canaanites. It is a bloody epic chapter in the family of Israel.

Israel will eventually take over the majority of their promised land. The Epic Marriage of Moses and Zipporah was essential to the epic plan of God. God was going to see His plan through no matter what happened. Since Moses and Zipporah were obedient to God and faithful to their spouse's well-being, they enjoyed the privilege of being an integral part of God's plan. An epic wife is essential to an Epic Marriage and in God's epic; an Epic Marriage is always used.

## Discussion Questions with Your Spouse or Small Group

*How does Peter (I Peter 3:1-4) tell women to show their husbands who Christ is?*

*Of these qualities, which is the hardest?*

*What can you do in your personal life to help develop these qualities?*

*What are some other ways you can protect you husband spiritually?*

# Chapter 6
# A Pursuing Husband:
# Ruth and Boaz

## A Family Lost a Nation Formed

Some will blend in and some will stand out. God must have known that as Israel took over Canaan they would fail to completely follow His instructions. His orders were clear. Be the only people group in your Promised Land. Yet, as Joshua led the family of Israel to take over Canaan some people groups were spared.

In those days, false gods were found in everything and were everywhere. The two most popular gods of the day were Baal and Ashereth. Baal was the god of weather and he was sometimes referred to as "the rider of the clouds." Then there was Ashereth, the goddess of fertility. In some cultures, she is seen as the wife of Baal. These two idols were the gods of the culture. Baal took care of the crops that provided wealth and Ashereth took care of the sex, which provided pleasure and descendants. As the Israelites settled in Canaan, they quickly forgot the mighty acts of God that saved them from slavery and delivered them out of the wilderness. Instead, many turned to the gods of a foreign culture as they identified with their new home.

Israel is now a nation. They have a common law in the Ten Commandments and they have a land in Canaan. They don't however have a king. Consequently, Israel fails to follow God and chose to worship false idols. God will send judges to deliver them from their self-induced bondage. It was during these spiritually tumultuous times we find a man and a woman solely committed to God. Instead of the rest of Israel, blending in with the culture around them, they will stand out in their worship of the one true Yahweh God. Because of their commitment to God, they too will have an opportunity to play a major role in the epic of God. In addition, because of their focus on God they provide a wonderful example of a healthy marriage in our material and sexually driven culture.

## Ruth

Ruth was a Moabite married to an Israelite. She married into an Israelite family that was seeking refuge from a famine in Moab. Ruth's would be father-in-law passed away before she was married to his son. After getting married, she moved in with her in-law near the lush fertile plains of Moab and began her new life. Now Naomi, Ruth's mother-in-law, is a widow in a foreign land. Naomi's only hope for survival in Moab is with her two sons and their new wives. It is not long when things turn worse for Naomi when her two sons die leaving Naomi with her two Moabite daughter-in-laws, Orpha and Ruth.

A widowed woman has very little opportunity in a foreign land. Naomi must now begin to make her way back to Israel. When she hears of God moving in Israel, she packs her things and begins her journey homeward. She turns to her two daughters-in-law and tells them to stay in Moab and to remarry. She prays a blessing over their lives and tries to leave. Ruth and

Orpha will not let Naomi leave without them. Naomi logically argues that they have no chance of marriage in her household if they stay with her. Orpha begins to agree with Naomi and chooses to stay in Moab. Ruth however, remains loyal to Naomi and she becomes a follower of the One True Yahweh God of Israel, thus returning with Naomi to Israel. Ruth, a Moabite woman is denying all she knows of home and religion to follow the one true God of Israel. Like Abraham, Ruth by faith will go to a land that she has never seen before to follow a God she never knew existed.

## Boaz

Boaz is a distant relative to Naomi from her husband's side of the family. This is important because Naomi's husband was from the tribe of Judah. This is important because in the book of Genesis Jacob blesses Judah and tells him that his bothers (the tribes of Israel) will worship him and the nations will follow him (Genesis 49:9-10). It becomes apparent that the Messiah will come from the Tribe of Judah. Thus, part of God's epic plan runs through the veins of Judah's DNA. Boaz is one of the Israelites that is from the tribe of Judah and chooses to maintain his worship of the One True God of Israel. God is going to use one of His faithful followers from the Tribe of Judah to continue the revelation of His epic.

The Scripture calls Boaz "a man of great wealth" (Ruth 2:1 NASB) or a "man of standing" (Ruth 2:1 NIV). The Hebrew word used here can also mean an influential person or war hero.[15] Either way, it should be understood that Boaz had a great reputation in his community. Scripture portrays Boaz as a strong and capable man who also has a tremendous trust in God. Who, oh-by-the-way happens to be single.

## They Meet

Ruth is now living in Bethlehem with Naomi. They are very poor, so Ruth sets out to go find food to help support her and her mother-in-law. She tells her that she is going to go and take the leftover crops from whomever she finds favor. This was a common practice for the poor in Jewish communities. In fact, Jesus does this in one of the Gospels. A corner portion of land was usually set apart for the poor to feed themselves. As Ruth is harvesting, she discovers that she is working in a field owned by Boaz. As Boaz is making the rounds of his property, Ruth catches his eye. He inquires of her and the Book of Ruth wastes no time in revealing the patient pursuit of Boaz in making Ruth his wife.

In the following pages, I would like to look at the patient and pursuing qualities of Boaz to help us men consider what it means to be patient pursuers of our wives. If you are a man, you may be saying, "Well I already have her? Why do I need to pursue her?" Your wife always wants you to pursue her. Every woman wants to be chased. She wants to know that you are still working for her, longing only for her, and that she is still on the front burners of your mind. "Well, if that's how she really feels why does she treat me like ---- or why doesn't she try to look like she did before we got married..." In the last chapter when I encouraged epic wives to respect their husbands, they asked themselves the same questions in their own way.

Before you were married, you worked hard at earning your future bride's respect. It was part of the package. You sent flowers, you bought jewelry, and you kept your house or apartment clean. When you got married, you forgot where the flower shop was and how to put your shoes in the closet. Your pursuit and your desire for her respect dwindled not on purpose, but just because that is how a man is wired. I would like for us to be re-wired. In fact, I think it is essential that epic husbands work daily at re-wiring their brains to pursue and cherish that which they have already gained. It is absolutely essential to your role in living out an Epic Marriage because Jesus provides for us men the greatest example of how to love our wives. No matter what the church does or looks like, Jesus continues to pursue her and give her His love. We too must reflect Christ to the bride He has given us.

## Surrender

The first patient pursuing manly characteristic we see of Boaz is in his commitment to God. Scripture makes it clear that God's intentions come first in his work and daily decisions. In the first occasion we see that he greets his workers with a blessing from God, "Now behold, Boaz came from Bethlehem and said to the reapers, "May the LORD be with you." And they said to him, "May the LORD bless you" (Ruth 2:4). He was not afraid to bring God into the workplace.

He does it again to a total stranger. It is Ruth this time, but he only knows her as a poor woman picking up the leftover crops in his field. To her he says, "May the LORD reward your work, and your wages be full from the LORD, the God of Israel, under whose wings you have come to seek refuge" (Ruth 2:12). This was a stranger. He did not have to speak to this woman. In fact, it would have been more appropriate not to do so. She is a poor Jewish woman working in a field. He is a wealthy landowner with lots of big important things to do. Yet he takes time for those who are less fortunate than he to bless and affirm their lives.

This is the first characteristic epic husbands must embrace—a complete surrender to God in our daily lives. If most men would just begin to surrender to God, it would drastically change the landscape of most American homes and churches. What part of your life are you fearful of letting God take from you? It is a nebulous question to say the least. How do you know if something is surrendered to God? I think the answer is found in your response to this scenario: What are you willing to do to keep whatever it is you have—possessions, status, or influence? If your answer is anything, you have not surrendered these things to the Lord. Let me define "anything." Are you willing to do something you know without a shadow of doubt is against God's command in Scripture in order to keep whatever it is you have? Are you willing to lie to keep it? Are you willing to steal to keep it? Are you will to cheat to keep it? Because the bottom line is, God may one day demand whatever it is you have. Your family, job, lifestyle, status, car, boat, or houses are all up for grabs in God's economy. If you are willing to stay true to God and lose all of those things, you are a surrendered man. Now many of you may be surprised to learn that by these standards you have surrendered you life to God. My next question is, "Can anyone tell?"

Boaz was surrendered to God. It was obvious to his employees and the citizens in his community that he was a godly man. Why? Well, the only few examples we have are what he *said* and Who he attributes all blessings to. What phrases are found on your lips? Boaz doesn't show a lot of wit, or at least Scripture doesn't care to point it out. He is not rubbing shoulders with the right people making crass jokes or boasting about his accomplishments. He is a man who lets his hard work speak for itself and he is not afraid to give God the glory for his accomplishments. He is also not a socially dysfunctional guy. He is well-liked and respected by those who know him. So much so, Naomi is going to work very hard to get

Ruth hooked up with him. Ruth who seems not too worried about men and status is just as infatuated with Boaz. Surrender is not a manly word. In fact, we are taught as young men not to surrender. War heroes never surrender. If it is fourth and short, go for it, never give up what you have already won. If we want to live, if we want a chance to win the game later or to experience the joy of doing what's right, we must surrender. Don't fear the word. There is nothing wrong with surrendering to the God of the universe. Trust God by surrendering to Him all He has commanded from you. Don't waste another day thinking your way is better. God has a deep profound unquenchable love for you. Rest in that love and know His very best waits for you in surrender.

My son hates to sleep. He is very social and he never wants to miss anything. In his room, we have a blue chair and a sound machine. He knows when we sit in the blue chair with the sound machine on, it is time to go to sleep. With all his force, he will straighten out his back, lock his legs and cry. He will fight because he is tired, but he does not want to sleep. However, Mom and I know that if he doesn't sleep he will not get the rest he needs, he won't grow a strong body and mind, and he will be very grumpy later. We hold him close and reassure him that he is okay until finally he surrenders. He can't win. I laugh to myself sometimes that this little seventeen-pound baby boy is trying to fight a 210-pound man. There is no way he can win. He can buck and cry and I will continue to love him and gently cradle him until he surrenders. I am sure God must look at us the same way. He knows what we need is His rest and peace. Yet we think we know what's best for us so we lock up, buck and fight what we know deep down inside it's a winless battle. At the end of the day, God is going to get His way and if He doesn't, who really wins?

How do we learn to surrender? It is part study and part experience. We begin surrendering to God by learning about God. Don't try to live the Christian life without God's Word. Ingest some of the Bible every day. It is a perfect treasure of truth. It is something you can actually trust to be straightforward and honest with you. Make time reading the Bible a priority in your life. It is important that somehow you get alone with God and a Bible to evaluate you life and strengthen spiritually. This can't be done in a pew or a small group. There must be some point in your week when you and God have a talk "God to man" about your life and His will.

Secondly, you have to experience God's faithfulness. Men like results. I know I do. I don't know why, but for some reason it still shocks me every time I surrender an area of my life I have held from God. He is faithful to deliver. He met the need I thought would go unmet. He provided the job best for me, and He has provided the necessities of life that I knew I needed. Right now, you know what you have to surrender. Money, possessions, status—whatever it is you have. He can make it best. Life is richer when we surrender to its Author.

## Patient Pursuit

The love story of Ruth and Boaz continues. It turns out Boaz starts to gives Ruth special privileges while she is in his fields. She's allowed to pick alongside the workers of the fields and the workers will assist her as well. He also has Ruth over for an evening meal at the ranch. Ruth's mother-in-law, Naomi, realizes that Boaz must have feelings for Ruth to do this for her. She schemes up a plan to get Ruth in the right place at the right time to launch this relationship to a quick marriage. It is in this plan that we find Boaz's patient pursuit. A man going about his business goes out of his way to honor a woman who will soon be his wife. He is an epic man. As husbands, we need to take on these characteristics towards our wives as we wait on God and pursue them at the same time. Let the chase begin!

Naomi advises Ruth that for some reason, probably to protect his crops, Boaz will be spending the night at the threshing floor. She encourages Ruth to wash herself, put on freshly scented oils, put on her best tunic, go to the threshing floor and wait for him to eat his meal and be satisfied. When he goes to sleep, Ruth is to go and lay at his feet, in an act of submission, and commit to him to be his servant. Ruth does everything Naomi tells her to do. Imagine! Boaz was sleeping peacefully on a full tummy of fajitas (not really, but you get the idea) when he feels something rustling at his feet. He jumps up, disoriented, and frightened, "Who are you?" he asks.

Then a little gentle familiar voice sounds in the darkness, "I am Ruth, your maid." She then asks Boaz to spread his covering over her because he is her kinsman redeemer.

A kinsman redeemer system was established in the book of Leviticus early in Israel's history. It required that the closest relative was to take care of a deceased man's possessions or a poor man's needs. In this case, Boaz was to take Ruth as his wife to redeem her as the closest relative to her husband. Essentially, Ruth was surrendering to marry Boaz. She didn't have to do this. All Boaz had to do was take care of Naomi. Boaz knows this and is honored by her request. He says, "May you be blessed of the LORD, my daughter. You have shown your last kindness to be better than the first by not going after young men, whether poor or rich. Now, my daughter, do not fear. I will do for you whatever you ask, for all my people in the city know that you are a woman of excellence" (Ruth 3:10-11). The first characteristic of this soon-to-be epic husband is he recognizes his bride's character and praises her for it.

When was the last time you praised your wife for something other than her body? Men are visual and it is natural for us to tell our wives how great they look. I am by no means saying you should stop doing that. In fact, you may need to start again, but what about her character, her personality, her passion in life? Have ever you told your wife you are proud of her walk with God? Have you ever overheard someone talking highly about your wife and then reported it to her to affirm her? These are all things epic husbands do! We must take time to praise our wives. If we ever hope to lead our homes, it does not start with strength, it starts with the humility of surrendering to God and praising our wife. Begin now taking note of who your wife is and what she does and magnify her good traits by praising her. For some of you this is natural; for the other 99% of us it is not. We will have to start by making a conscious effort and be reminded later. Nevertheless, she will respect you and live up to every blessing you speak over her life.

The next quality Boaz shows is his integrity. He knows that he is not the closest relative. "Now it is true I am a close relative; however, there is a relative closer than I. Remain this night, and when morning comes, if he will redeem you, good; let him redeem you. But if he does not wish to redeem you, then I will redeem you, as the LORD lives. Lie down until morning" (Ruth 3:12-13). Boaz is obviously attracted to Ruth. How many of us would have shown this much patience? Yet Boaz knows that God's way is best, so he embraces it and he asks Ruth to as well.

Could you lead your wife this way? Are you in a position morally to help your family know and achieve God's best? Boaz is a man of integrity. Leadership in the home requires integrity. Integrity is best defined by the things you do when no one else is watching. No one is watching Boaz and Ruth right now. In fact they could have consummated the whole deal right there on the threshing floor. However, Boaz honors his wife-to-be and wants God's best for her, so he waits to do things God's way. How is your private life? If we hope to lead our families, we must know how to do things God's way in our own lives first so we will know how to do it for our families when the occasion arises.

The final characteristic of an epic husband we see in Boaz is he protects his wife-to-be.

*So she lay at his feet until morning and rose before one could recognize another; and he said, "Let it not be known that the woman came to the threshing floor."*

*Again he said, "Give me the cloak that is on you and hold it." So she held it, and he measured six measures of barley and laid it on her. Then she went into the city (Ruth 3:14-15).*

Boaz protects Ruth physically and her reputation through the night. Boaz is protecting his barley crop, so one could assume that the threshing floor is no place for a woman to be walking alone in the middle of the night. Instead of sending her back to the house, he tells her to sleep at his feet until morning comes. The sentence closes with a warning about her reputation, "Let it not be known that the woman came to the threshing floor." Her actions could be misunderstood tarnishing an excellent reputation.

I hope it is your natural inclination to protect your wife physically. You are not her equal. You are bigger and stronger than she is and God has put you in her life to protect her as He would. Never complain about going through the steps required to make your wife feel safe at night. Don't overdue it and scare her to death, but at the same time, if she is frightened you have one job—protection. This is a natural instinct for most men. However, look for ways to go out of your way to watch over her. Your wife may be the type who is too kind to ask, so think like a bodyguard. What possible scenarios endanger your wife? If she must have late nights at the office or late nights out shopping, if possible, go with her or meet her at the door when it is time for her to come home. Have her car equipped with basic safety necessities in case she is ever stranded and you are not with her. Think about any and every possible scenario in how you can protect you wife and then take whatever steps you can to ensure her safety.

What about protecting her reputation? What have you done for her reputation lately? Maybe you have used it as an opportunity to make you look better than her, or to be funny with the guys. An epic husband does no such thing. Look for any occasion to promote your wife's excellence in public. Too often, I hear men bashing their wives verbally behind their backs so they seem smart, funny, or witty. Even if she never finds out, God knows and it is in your heart. This is not your role in her life. You should be her best cheerleader.

I remember having lunch with an agnostic friend one day. We had been meeting together for a over a year to talk about the existence of God. After about a year, God showed up in his life, but my friend wasn't ready to surrender to Jesus as Lord. Despite his strides in belief, he could not bring himself to trust in Christ as Savior. This grieved his wife. As a believer, she wanted her husband to know the richness she had discovered in Christ. That night after he and I had lunch, his wife came over to talk to Angie. As she commonly did, his wife inquired of me how lunch went with her husband. I told her some of the details about where he was spiritually, but I was proud to tell her that in my conversation with her husband he was always quick to praise her. I told her, "He loves you, he thinks you're the best thing that ever happened to him." You should have seen her face light up. I will never forget her expression. The next night she went home after a women's Bible study and boldly told him she was going to walk with him in Christ and that is was time for him for trust in Christ as Savior. He became a Christian that night.

You never know who is going to tell your wife what you say about her behind her back. I want my wife to know my love for her wherever she turns. If it's home or in public, I want people to know without a shadow of doubt that I love my wife and that she is the second best thing that ever happened to me. I love her work ethic. I love her passion for our children. I love her desire to know God. I love her simple faith. I love her heart for the hurting. I love her desire to be there for me no matter what. I love her passion for sports. I love her smile and the way her eyes catch me when I do something great or when I say something stupid. I love my wife! Go ahead and make your own list. I am no Romeo, Shakespeare, or Richard Marx, but I know this: I love my wife. I know that my words have more impact in her life than anyone else's. I can tear her down or I can build her up. God wants me to build her up. If He wants to fix something in Angie, He will fix it. My job is not to fix my wife, but to love my wife. Unconditionally, unquenchably, uncontrollably love my wife, my Angie, my bride. Go now and be epic in your love for your wife. Let it no insecurity or selfish promotion stand in the way of a passionate epic love for your wife.

## The Epic Point

The book of Ruth is four chapters long. It tells the story of a woman and man who fall in love and by divine providence get married. It turns out that the closest relative to Ruth could not afford her. Boaz received his prize, a wife of excellence. Through Boaz and Ruth, the line of Judah continues. Their epic purpose was to have children in the Lord. Ruth and Boaz have Obed, which means "worshiper." Obed grows up in the Lord and has a son named Jesse. Jesse grows and becomes the father of eight sons. During the life of Jesse, Israel decides they want a king. God gives them what they want with a warning that a king will come with a price. Israel's first appointed King is Saul. King Saul starts his reign well, but eventually he begins to fail in the eyes of God. God appoints another king. King David is chosen as a young boy still tending the sheep for his father Jesse. Ruth and Boaz are part of King David's legacy. King David will be the greatest king Israel has ever known. Israel will long for another king like King David. Finally, God delivers Israel's final king, Jesus Christ, through the line of Ruth and Boaz and King David.

An Epic Marriage is worth surrender. An Epic Marriage is worth humility. An Epic Marriage is worth sacrificing all that you are to love your spouse, just as Christ did for us on the cross. An epic purpose demands an epic sacrifice. There may be no easier way to ensure Christ is at the center of your marriage than to be a living sacrifice in your marriage. Go surrender, protect, guide and love your wife.

## Discussion Questions with Your Spouse or Small Group

*How can we live out our faith in God as Boaz did?*

*What encourages the faith of a man?*

*Take a second right now and praise God for your wife's character.*

*What is the best way to praise your wife's character?*

*Define integrity. What does it look like today?*

*How can you protect and provide for your wife today?*

# Chapter 7
# Epic Failure

## An Epic King: David and Bathsheba

Israel wanted a king. God gave Israel what they demanded in King Saul. King Saul ruled with an insecure heart and for little regard of God's desire for His nation. Through a series of events, God removes King Saul from leadership and replaces him with King David, son of Jesse. The Bible says King David was a man after God's own heart. He was a powerful king. He spread the influence of Israel by military strength, conquering competing nations. Under King David's leadership, Israel rose to become a world superpower.

Not only was King David a military genius, King David was a visionary. As a visionary, he had a passion to rebuild the Temple of God. David begins forging plans to build the temple and God sends the prophet Nathan to stop him. God tells David that it would not be appropriate for a man who has killed so many people build the Temple of God. This deeply disappoints David. However, God has something else in mind for David.

Abraham was the last person God spoke directly to concerning the epic arrival of the Messiah. Now hundreds of years later, God adds a second chapter to His epic covenant with the people of Israel through their beloved King David of the tribe of Judah.

*"I will give you rest from all your enemies. The LORD also declares to you that the LORD will make a house for you. When your days are complete and you lie down with your fathers, I will raise up your descendant after you, who will come forth from you, and I will establish his kingdom. He shall build a house for My name, and I will establish the throne of his kingdom forever. I will be a father to him and he will be a son to Me; when he commits iniquity, I will correct him with the rod of men and the strokes of the sons of men, but My loving kindness shall not depart from him, as I took it away from Saul, whom I removed from before you. Your house and your kingdom shall endure before Me forever; your throne shall be established forever" ( II Samuel 7:11-16).*

God makes a covenant with David. First, He tells David that he will have rest from all his enemies. This promised rest eventually comes late in his life. David's rest from his enemies paves the way for his son, King Solomon, to lead Israel during a time of great peace. Second, God promises David that his son will build the Holy Temple of God. David's son Solomon will continue to spread the influence of Israel, making Israel a larger more powerful nation through trading, intermarriage, and economy. God tells King David that He will lead his son and will never remove His hand from his son's life. God will faithfully correct Solomon and will have unending grace with Solomon when he fails.

Finally, God promises David that David's throne will be established forever. This part of the covenant reaches into eternity. There is only one way for this part of the covenant to be fulfilled. If God plans to establish David's throne forever, then an eternal King must come through the lineage of King

David of the tribe of Judah. Therefore, Jesus Christ the Messiah and King is the fulfillment of this covenant. This makes David an Epic King! King David's purpose was to faithfully lead the nation of Israel to follow God, to have a child that will one day take his place as king, and to continue the epic family line of Abraham that will one day link to Christ.

David is faithful to his purpose. Until one beautiful spring day when the Bible says kings went off to war, David stayed home. After a nice long afternoon nap, King David wakes up to a gentle spring breeze blowing in the curtains of his room. He stands up, stretches, and slowly walks out the patio door of his sleeping chamber to smell the fresh air and cedar after a refreshing nap. From the top of the palace, he can look over all of Jerusalem. He can see into the wilderness towards his borders. He swells with the satisfaction of all the Lord has accomplished through him. His eyes begin to move down towards the streets to see the people trading in the market, kids being called in for supper, and then his eyes are suddenly stopped. His heart races, he can feel his face turn flush. He can't help but to stare. She's so beautiful. His heart continues to race. "I can't stop looking at her," he says to himself. His mouth becomes dry as he continues to visually inhale the perfectly tanned, toned woman taking a bath on her rooftop. Every part of her body is on display for the king to indulge.

Caught up in the lust of the moment, King David calls out to his advisors to find out who the woman is. It turns out that her name is Bathsheba and her husband is off fighting in the war that David chose not to attend. The lust is taken a step further. He sends messengers to "take her" back to his palace. That night David, a married man, takes Bathsheba, a married woman, and has sex with her. The seriousness of this event cannot be overstated. The penalty for adultery was death according to the Book of Leviticus (20:10). Not only is the penalty steep, but his reasoning is ridiculous. In crass manly terms, King David had multiple wives and concubines. He could have slept with a different woman every night of the week. They never said no, they were never too tired and had no headaches. If one was unable to have sex with David, he could just go to the next woman down the hall. It goes to show that having everything is still not enough.

Just as some weak followers of Christ do, David and Bathsheba bluntly sin against God. Despite their adultery, Bathsheba still practices the Leviticus requirements of cleanliness after intercourse. They only obey the part of God's law that does not affect their pleasure. After Bathsheba considers herself clean, she returns home. Weeks later, Bathsheba sends a message to David. "I am pregnant." David does not seem to miss a beat. He immediately inquires of her husband's whereabouts and puts into plan a way for him to come home and sleep with Bathsheba so that the baby will appear to be his. Brilliant! This is way before DNA testing and what man who's been away fighting in a war would not give anything to come home and sleep with his wife?

Bathsheba's husband, Uriah, was the type of guy who would not sleep with his wife on a brief visit home from war. Why? Good question, he is a better man than I am. It seems Uriah is a man who honors and respects his fellow soldiers. He was not going to enjoy the pleasures of home while his friends suffered in battle. Therefore, he slept outside King David's house to protect the king! The Bible does a great job of painting a stark contrast between these two men.

In the thickness of David's blindness, he believes he had no choice. After a few days at home, David sends Uriah back to the battlefield with a sealed note. When Uriah arrives at the battle, his commanding officer opens the note and follows its instructions. He orders Uriah to lead the next charge as the army of Israel pulls away. The result is a quick painful death of Uriah, the faithful husband of Bathsheba and faithful soldier of King David. Now David has committed two sins—adultery and murder. As Bathsheba mourns her husband's death David seeks to comfort her.

A few months pass by and David marries Bathsheba and she gives birth to a son. Then God intervenes.

Years before these events, the prophet Nathan risked his life to anoint David as the King of Israel during the reign of King Saul. Nathan was a trusted advisor to King David and clearly spoke for God. Nathan arrives at David's house to deliver a message of judgment.

*Thus says the LORD, "Behold, I will raise up evil against you from your own household; I will even take your wives before your eyes and give them to your companion, and he will lie with your wives in broad daylight. Indeed you did it secretly, but I will do this thing before all Israel, and under the sun" (2 Samuel 12:11-12).*

God delivers a drawn-out dreadful punishment because of David's sin. David's son, Absalom, will rise up against him in later days and take the throne from his father for a brief period. Absalom will also sleep with his father's wives. The whole nation will watch and some will even support the disrespectful acts that will occur in the twilight of David's reign. Eventually, against David's wishes, Absalom will be killed in a battle to retake the throne. Nathan informs David that before these events take place, the son conceived in adultery will not survive. However, David's life will be spared because God has forgiven his sin. David fasted and prayed many days and nights for the child. However, his first son with Bathsheba passes away after seven days.

Before you start developing a theology of sin, abortion, and God's retributive acts, please take time to read the New Testament. What God does to David for his sins are specific to David's situation and sin. A good rule for reading the Bible is not to make grand theological claims based on single events in Scripture. You know God by knowing the entire Bible. Many children are conceived out of adulterous relationships and they are going to be just fine. In fact, some have become preachers, leaders and great contributors to society. God is in the business of forgiveness and restoration. The Biblical portrayal of God's retributive acts are far less frequent than His acts of restoration.

## Marital Sin

I hope and pray that the events of this chapter and the next never take place in your marriage. Statistically speaking 5% (1 out of 20) of men will cheat on their wives. If 100 men buy this book, five of them have or eventually will cheat on their wives, statistically speaking.[16] In the same study it was reported that 4.55% of wives will commit adultery as well.[17] In *Oprah* magazine 15% of women reported that they had committed adultery on their spouse. So if 100 people buy this book anywhere from ten to twenty of them has or will commit adultery.

Adultery is not the only sin of marriage. Marriage is a covenant of faithfulness. Anything that can be understood as unfaithful is a sin against your marriage. One could lump pornography or any stage of lust in with the sins against a spouse (Matthew 5:27-28). However, there are more sins.

Lying is rampant in marriage. Lying, unresolved bitterness, an emotional connection with the opposite sex, flirting with the opposite sex, gossiping about your spouse, hurtful words, purposefully withholding sexual fulfillment and more are all sins against marriage. When you married your spouse, you committed your life to his or her growth and maturity in the Lord. Anything that distracts, hurts, or interferes with that purpose is a strike against marriage and God. Some sins against a marriage just sting more. Sins like adultery are worse than others are in our human economy.

If your marriage is experiencing an epic killing sin, I want to encourage you to take things slowly when comes to ending your marriage. It takes two to kill a marriage and two to restore a marriage. I believe David makes the right steps when it comes to beginning the process of an offending spouse's restoration. If you are in need of restoration, or have a marriage that is in need of restoration, this chapter and the next chapter will be essential to your Epic Marriage. It is possible to be restored back to a right relationship with each other and God. I believe in these situations God gets the most glory from a couple who decides to embrace the grace of Jesus and forgive one another versus the opposite.

## I Confess

After David realizes his sin, he confesses to Nathan. The first thing a failing spouse must do as he or she realizes their sin is confess. Confession is a funny thing in church life. Depending on what denomination you are coming from, you may have a different view on confession. Catholics would confess to a priest. A Baptist might confess only to God. Those who follow Jesus Christ as Lord know they are to confess to Christ and then to the one they offended.

Jesus spoke of this when He said:

*Therefore if you are presenting your offering at the altar, and there remember that your brother has something against you, leave your offering there before the altar and go; first be reconciled to your brother, and then come and present your offering (Matthew 5:23-24).*

Jesus warns His followers, if we sin against someone, it is important that we ask for forgiveness from that person before we worship God. Jesus would say that it is just as important that you confess to God and to those you have offended. In the case of marriage, if we ever hope to be free from the sins that enslave us, we must expose our sin to light by confessing to our spouse.

Confession is a powerful tool when it comes to the power of sin. If you will trust God's grace and utilize it, you will find extraordinary freedom. Many spouses fear confession. They fear what their spouse will do or how they will respond. My only warning is that eventually your sin will be revealed. Sins that damage marriages start secretive. Eventually the person you are married to will be able to see the difference in you. The sin will become such a large part of your identity you will not be able to hide it any longer. Eventually the computer history will tell the story. Eventually the news around the office makes its way home. Eventually the sin will come and find those you love the most.

The question is not, "How will they respond?" The better question is, "How should they find out?" One day you come home and your spouse is weeping at the couch, or you go to a party and that certain person is there. It is better to confess and repent. Make a commitment and take steps never to do the sin again. Find a friend who can hold you accountable. Sever the unholy relationship dragging you down. Disconnect the cable and throw out the computer. Do whatever it takes to make your sin impossible. Then ask your spouse for their forgiveness. Praise God for His forgiveness that already covers you.

# Restored

After Nathan reveals David's sin, he is told that his son will die. This is terrible news for everyone involved. No one wants to see this child die. The baby is removed from what may have been a devastating situation and is nestled in the arms of God. In the midst of the baby's sickness, David dresses in sackcloth. He fasts and prays to God for the baby's survival. It is too late. God has already decided how long this child will live. He brings him home to glory after seven days. After the baby dies, David puts on his royal garments and has a meal prepared. David is comforted by the fact that he knows he will one day see the boy again and he tells his servants he is done fasting. "But now he has died; why should I fast? Can I bring him back again? I will go to him, but he will not return to me" (II Samuel 12:23).

We can learn a lot from David in these moments. Possibly seven months after the rebuke of Nathan, David is aware of his relationship with God. He knows that God loves Him and David has not continued in the sin of adultery. David knows and lives as a restored life unto God.

Some epic sins are so damaging to the spirit of a person that they struggle with receiving forgiveness. As I said earlier, God is in the business of restoration. Your sin is forgiven and God has already forgiven you for your next sin. It is a lie from Satan that you are not forgiven. Despaired, bitter, and separated from God is right where the enemy wants you. Receive His grace and continue in your relationship with the Father.

For some this process is more difficult than for others. Depending on your personality and spiritual giftedness, you can receive God's forgiveness easier than others can. I was recently working with a young man who made a very poor decision that almost cost him his marriage. I told him to read Psalm 51 everyday. As far as I know, he is still reading it. I believe reading and praying God's Word over your life will help bring about spiritual healing and comfort through your sorrow and conviction of sin, no matter who you are.

Receiving God's grace is essential to your restoration. Wallowing in pity earns you no favor with God. Receive His sufficient grace and experience a restored relationship with Him. The sooner you began to walk with God, the sooner you will find peace again. There will be consequences, but at least you will know you are now where God wants you; with Him.

Finally, when it comes to restoration, don't to try to do it alone. David had Nathan and Bathsheba who supported him through this process. Be sure you find a trusted friend or pastor who will pray with you, for you, and speak grace into your life. You will need strong companions for what will be a long journey towards peace.

# Renewed

David wrote Psalm 51 after Nathan rebuked him concerning the affair he had with Bathsheba. In the psalm, King David asks God, "Restore to me the joy of Your salvation and sustain me with a willing spirit. Then I will teach transgressors Your ways, and sinners will be converted to You" (Psalm 51:12-13). David's goal in restoration was to help others not make the same mistakes. To me this is seeing your cup as half full. You have let God, your family and everyone else down. However, you will get through this and when you do you will help others to not follow in your path.

Broken men and women have started some of the greatest ministries the church has ever known. I think God loves sinners. Not only that, but He loves to use sinners too. That is the Good News of Jesus Christ. God loves you and has plans to make you holy. Ask yourself whom you can help. Allow God to use this dreadful experience to help His followers. Doing this does not make up for your sin. That is not necessary, but helping others will help ease the sting of sin's consequences.

As we move to the next chapter, I want you prayerfully to read Psalm 51. Allow God's Word to take root in your life and shape your next steps. Even if this chapter does not apply to you, it will not hurt to consider every precious word in prayer.

*Be gracious to me, O God, according to Your loving kindness;*
*According to the greatness of Your compassion blot out my transgressions.*
*Wash me thoroughly from my iniquity*
*And cleanse me from my sin.*
*For I know my transgressions,*
*And my sin is ever before me.*
*Against You, You only, I have sinned*
*And done what is evil in Your sight,*
*So that You are justified when You speak*
*And blameless when You judge.*
*Behold, I was brought forth in iniquity,*
*And in sin my mother conceived me.*
*Behold, You desire truth in the innermost being,*
*And in the hidden part You will make me know wisdom.*
*Purify me with hyssop, and I shall be clean;*

*Wash me, and I shall be whiter than snow.*
*Make me to hear joy and gladness,*
*Let the bones which You have broken rejoice.*
*Hide Your face from my sins*
*And blot out all my iniquities.*
*Create in me a clean heart, O God,*
*And renew a steadfast spirit within me.*
*Do not cast me away from Your presence*
*And do not take Your Holy Spirit from me.*
*Restore to me the joy of Your salvation*
*And sustain me with a willing spirit.*
*Then I will teach transgressors Your ways,*
*And sinners will be converted to You.*
*Deliver me from blood guiltiness, O God, the God of my*
*salvation;*
*Then my tongue will joyfully sing of Your righteousness.*
*O Lord, open my lips,*
*That my mouth may declare Your praise.*
*For You do not delight in sacrifice, otherwise I would give it;*
*You are not pleased with burnt offering.*
*The sacrifices of God are a broken spirit; A broken and a*
*contrite heart, O God, You will not despise.*
*By Your favor do good to Zion;*
*Build the walls of Jerusalem.*
*Then You will delight in righteous sacrifices,*
*In burnt offering and whole burnt offering;*
*Then young bulls will be offered on Your altar (Psalm 51).*

# Chapter 8
# Epic Grace, Epic Genealogy

## Hosea and Gomer

I hope Austin or one of my sons is a star quarterback for a Big Twelve College and uses his influence to spread the Gospel. I hope Audrey is brilliant and becomes a physician and a missionary, and helps individuals in third world nations to find healing, physically and spiritually. I hope great and lofty things for my kids. What parent doesn't? Imagine if God told you that your great-great-great-great-grandchild was going to be the Savior of humanity. You would say, "Well only a real holy person could receive this kind of legacy?"

"Not so fast," God would say. "My grace is sufficient to provide such a legacy for even the worst of sinners."

God takes pleasure in restoration. I think God enjoys using broken, desperate individuals to do epic events through case in point, the genealogy of Jesus Christ. Every event since Adam and Eve has been leading up to the revelation of humanity's ultimate need for salvation and its Savior. God took the broken sinful lives of individuals and gave them the ultimate restoration by including their names in the genealogy of His perfect Son Jesus Christ.

The record of the genealogy of Jesus the Messiah, the son of David, the son of Abraham:

*Abraham was the father of Isaac, Isaac the father of Jacob, and Jacob the father of Judah and his brothers. Judah was the father of Perez and Zerah by Tamar, Perez was the father of Hezron, and Hezron the father of Ram. Ram was the father of Amminadab, Amminadab the father of Nahshon, and Nahshon the father of Salmon. Salmon was the father of Boaz by Rahab, Boaz was the father of Obed by Ruth, and Obed the father of Jesse. Jesse was the father of David the king. David was the father of Solomon by Bathsheba who had been the wife of Uriah. Solomon was the father of Rehoboam, Rehoboam the father of Abijah, and Abijah the father of Asa. Asa was the father of Jehoshaphat, Jehoshaphat the father of Joram, and Joram the father of Uzziah. Uzziah was the father of Jotham, Jotham the father of Ahaz, and Ahaz the father of Hezekiah. Hezekiah was the father of Manasseh, Manasseh the father of Amon, and Amon the father of Josiah. Josiah became the father of Jeconiah and his brothers, at the time of the deportation to Babylon. After the deportation to Babylon: Jeconiah became the father of Shealtiel, and Shealtiel the father of Zerubbabel. Zerubbabel was the father of Abihud, Abihud the father of Eliakim, and Eliakim the father of Azor. Azor was the father of Zadok, Zadok the father of Achim, and Achim the father of Eliud. Eliud was the father of Eleazar, Eleazar the father of Matthan, and Matthan the father of Jacob. Jacob was the father of Joseph the husband of Mary, by whom Jesus was born, who is called the Messiah (Matthew 1:1-16).*

I hope that by now you are beginning to the see the epic. All of these couples make up the earthly legacy of Jesus Christ the Messiah. Genealogy was a big deal to the Israelites. Who your parents were said a lot about you. Therefore, what does this list say about Jesus? Abraham lied and doubted God's provision, so he slept with a slave girl to have children, but he was eventually obedient. Isaac lied like his father. Jacob deceived his father to steal his older brother's birthright. Perez had sex with a prostitute who turned out to be his own daughter. David lusted after a woman, slept with her, and killed her husband. Eventually he repented. Solomon was the son of David and Bathsheba. Solomon eventually turned his back on God and worshiped the gods of his many wives. Rehoboam was the son of Solomon who split the nation of Israel because of his pride. The list goes on to describe men and women who failed to live up to God's best for their lives.

This list tells me a lot. First, it tells me that the Bible was not manmade. No man would create a religion and a Messiah's heritage with so many character flaws. Secondly, it tells me that God is about His glory through His grace. God loves to dispense His grace. Many of us wonder what God can do with our lives after we have made such messes of them through our sin. God doesn't wonder about it. He knows exactly where He wants you in His epic. It is going to be by His grace, empowerment, and healing that you fulfill all that He has for you. The result will be the peace of knowing that your marriage and life counted for more than memories and trust funds. It counted for a legacy and for the betterment of humanity through the revelation of Jesus Christ.

What if you're the victim of a sinful spouse? It is not your fault. They failed you. Now they want your forgiveness. Now they want your commitment that you will stay with them through the healing process. Now they want you to be a tool God can use to restore them. What will you decide? How can you help someone who has hurt you so deeply? I can't convince you to ignore your feelings. They are honest and legitimate hurts. I can assure you that if you choose to stay, if you choose to be a part of restoring this individual, you will be better for it. If they are truly repentant and they are not physically hurting you in any way, I want to encourage you to remain in their lives as the spouse God can use to restore this person and your marriage to its epic potential.

Your marriage is not the first marriage to go through the sinful failure of a partner. You know that. But did you know there is a very significant marriage in the Old Testament that God commands the couple to stay together even after multiple adulterous relationships occurred? They are not in the genealogy of Christ, but I believe they are essential to God's epic because they are a testimony to His grace and restoration of the nation of Israel. Keep reading and my hope is that you will be encouraged and maybe discover what your next step is in the journey of restoring a repentant spouse.

## Hosea and Gomer

God spoke to a prophet named Hosea 760 years before Christ. He lived in Israel as a prophet against the pursuit of idols. God asked Hosea to make his life a living testimony to convict Israel of their sins. God commands Hosea to get married.

"Not a bad idea," Hosea might have said. "I've been thinking a wife might be a good thing."

God replies, "Hosea, you should know I want you to marry a prostitute."

"I'm sorry. God, I didn't quite catch that, did you say prostitute?" Hosea replies.

"Yes," God says, "I want you to marry a woman who has known other men the way you will know her. Nothing on her body will be sacred, nothing will be set apart for only you, and nothing about her will be reserved for you. All of her secrets and all of her intimacy will have been shared with multiple men. She will continue to live life as a harlot. No intimate act will be reserved for you. Her lips, her skin, her eyes and her thoughts will all be shared with other men."

"Why, God? Why would you have me marry such a woman?" Hosea might have asked.

"Because, Hosea, you have been sent to deliver a message to the people of Israel. They have played the role of the harlot to me. I have loved them, cherished them and set them apart for great things, yet they seek other lovers in their false gods," God replies.

Hosea was obedient. He knowingly married Gomer, the prostitute. Hosea and Gomer had three children. The first son was named "May God sow," implying that God was going to punish Israel for her disobedience. The second child was a daughter named, "Not my people." It is possible "Not my people" was not even Hosea's child. She could have been the result of one of the affairs Gomer had while married to Hosea. The third child was another son named, "Not my people, not your God."

Gomer continues to live out her life as a prostitute. Scripture implies that other men allure her. She doesn't need the money. She doesn't need the companionship. She just wants more men. She wants the satisfaction of knowing she has it all. Yet in having it all, she loses everything.

As commanded, Hosea lets Gomer play the harlot while he stays home to raise the children and communicate the message of God. Eventually, Gomer's sexual addiction enslaves her to her masters. She becomes a slave woman. She is placed on the slave market to be sold to the next desperate man. God commands Hosea to purchase her from her sins. For fifteen shekels of silver and six-and-a-half bushels of barley, Hosea buys Gomer out of her prostitution. When they get home, Hosea sits down with his wife and he tells her that he is going to restore her and that she is to be a harlot no longer. Scripture says it ever so slightly that Hosea is going to continue to embrace Gomer and love her, but the catch is that she cannot have intimacy with another man. Hosea is to be the only intimate partner in her life.

The prophecy of Hosea suggests that she repents. In the final chapter of the prophesy, God puts Himself in the role of Husband to Israel. God, through Hosea and Gomer's relationship, tells Israel how she will be restored. The book of Hosea is a powerful testimony to the significance marriage plays in relaying the message of God. Marriage is the only earthly relationship that comes close to being an example of the kind of relationship we have with God. This makes sense because marriage is a covenant. Covenants are not to be broken. God made a covenant with us through the death of His Son. By His very nature, God cannot break this covenant. He has to love us and He has already spiritually restored us. All we have to do is receive it through Christ.

Your marriage is a testimony to the greatness of God. If your spouse has come to you as a Gomer begging for your restoration, by the power of God, begin the process of helping your spouse find peace again. You may discover that in the process you are both healed. Because let's face it, you're both hurting. If you end the marriage, you just take the unresolved hurt with you, leaving no avenue or hope to resolve what has been broken. Just as God received you, now is the time to extended grace to your spouse and begin the journey of healing.

# The Journey of Healing

Healing takes time. The hurter and the hurting both need time for healing to take place. That is why healing is a journey. If you choose to embark on the blessed process of restoring a wayward spouse, realize that it will take time. In addition, do not be alarmed if it takes time before you feel up to making the journey. Allow for some time and a whole lot of prayer to cover you so you can approach the situation with a clear mind. Do not make a rash decision based on emotions. If you do, you run the risk of never having the opportunity to choose what may very well be God's epic purpose for your marriage.

## Admit Failure

Did you notice that communication is key when it comes to receiving and dispensing grace? King David had to confess with his lips that he failed God. Those of you who choose to help to restore a spouse need to be prepared to communicate about the very things your spouse did. Details are not necessary, but emotions and future actions need to be discussed. At the end of the Book of Hosea, God promises Israel restoration. The first thing God tells Israel to do is to communicate their failure.

*Return, O Israel, to the LORD your God, for you have stumbled because of your iniquity. Take words with you and return to the LORD. Say to Him, "Take away all iniquity and receive us graciously, that we may present the fruit of our lips" (Hosea 14:1-3).*

Words are essential to restoration. I do not know what questions need to be asked. I don't know what needs to be discussed, but I do know that sin needs to be exposed to light.

When we take sin from deep inside our hearts and expose it to the light of confession, it begins to die. If your spouse has sinned against you he or she needs to tell you so they can be forgiven and begin the process of healing.

When it comes to love and sin, details are not always best. Do not ask for them. A failed spouse should protect their loved one by being overly cautious with what is revealed. You may find the best conversations are the ones that deal with present feelings. How are things going to be different? What has changed in you that tells me you don't want to do this anymore? What were you feeling towards me when you were doing these things? How can I help you? Those are safe, hard questions every spouse should ask if they hope to help the restoration process.

## Free Grace

*I will heal their apostasy, I will love them freely, for My anger has turned away from them (Hosea 14:4).*

A second characteristic of God's restoration is His commitment to restoration and free grace towards Israel. God loved Israel before sin, while they sinned, and after they sinned. God was looking for sincere hearts. If your spouse comes to you with a sincere heart of repentance, you have a glorious opportunity to join God and restore them by maintaining your commitment to them. Not everyone gets this opportunity. It is a blessing and a testimony to the strength of you marriage and to Christ.

When your spouse comes to you seeking forgiveness, you have an opportunity to love them freely. This is not easy. The person you love the most has betrayed you. None of us is innocent of betrayal. We have all betrayed God. It is through

Christ we are restored to a right relationship with God despite our betrayal. I believe in marriage, the least we can do for a repentant spouse is offer them the same love that was offered to us on the cross. Our culture does not support this kind of grace-led thinking. Thankfully our God does. Extend to your spouse the love of Christ. Be a graceful listener. Ask questions. Cry with them, share your hurts and reassure them with your words that you love them and want to help them get through this season of repentance. When we do this, God will provide you with incredible strength. It may even lead to one of the most incredible seasons of your marriage.

You don't have to judge or fix your spouse. As Christians, we believe that the Holy Spirit is dwelling in us. The Holy Spirit guides us and convicts us of sin. Instead of trying to fix a spouse, allow the great Healer to do His work in their lives. Begin praying for them. Be a stable force of secure Christ-like love in their life. As you do this, your spouse will begin what promises to be a successful journey to healing.

## Restored

*I will be like the dew to Israel; He will blossom like the lily,*
*And he will take root like the cedars of Lebanon. His shoots*
*will sprout,*
*And his beauty will be like the olive tree*
*And his fragrance like the cedars of Lebanon. Those who*
*live in his shadow*
*Will again raise grain,*
*And they will blossom like the vine.*
*His renown will be like the wine of Lebanon (Hosea 14:5-7).*

Israel is restored by God's gentle touch of healing and grace. Hosea describes the restoration of Israel's reputation. This will come about through Israel's repentance and God's faithfulness to His covenant with Israel as His holy nation. Her reputation will be completely restored through the birth of Jesus Christ by whom God will bless all the families of the earth. God never promised that Israel would be and stay a superpower. He did promise that He had an epic purpose for Israel and He planned to use the married couples of Israel to help create the seed that would one day crush Satan.

A wounded spouse has an amazing opportunity to show the world the love of God by restoring an offending spouse. An Epic Marriage is purposeful about revealing Christ. It would be understandable and typical of this world for you to divorce your husband or wife who may have hurt you. I completely understand why you might even feel this way. In fact, depending on the situation, other passages in the Bible support you thinking this way. Thankfully, God did not leave Israel and He will never leave us. I think there is something supernaturally graceful in forgiving a spouse and working through the restoration process. I have seen all kinds of separations. I have seen couples separate because of adultery. I have seen couples separate over little dumb things like unresolved conflict and boredom. In addition, I have seen some bad marriages. I have also seen a few couples who have embraced an extremely painful situation and tried to do what they believed best glorified God. Forgiveness and restoration will always glorify God before bitterness and divorce.

I pray that you will never have to experience what Hosea and Gomer experienced. In case you do, I pray and hope you will have the opportunity and the strength to have epic grace. Your life will be better for it. You marriage will be better for it. In addition, this world will come one couple closer to seeing the forgiveness Christ offers us every day.

# Discussion Questions with Your Spouse or Small Group

*Of the two of you, who is the most merciful? Why?*
*How important is forgiveness in marriage?*
*What are the dangers of not forgiving in marriage?*
*What does this marriage tell you about how God views sin?*
*Why is all sin considered to be like adultery to God?*

*How do we avoid admitting failure? Why do we avoid admitting failure? Why is it important we admit failure?*

*How can we encourage our spouses to grow spiritually after failure?*

*How can we restore our spouse's reputation?*

# Chapter 9
# Epic Family—Epic Redemption

About 2,000 years ago, Christ was born in the town of Bethlehem. He was born of the Virgin Mary in the line of Abraham. Jesus is the perfect Son of God. As perfectly divine, Jesus lived as a perfect man upon the earth and died on the cross. The Bible tells us that Christ's death on the cross was a final payment for the sins of humanity. Through faith in Christ, we can have a right relationship with God despite our sinful nature. After Christ's crucifixion on the third day, He rose from the dead. For a brief period of about seven weeks, Christ walked the earth, spoke to followers, and revealed himself to a select group of individuals.

On His final day before His ascension, Jesus Christ, Son of God and Savior of the world gave His followers a final command. Go and make disciples. Go tell others about me and my Glory. Tell the people of the world that there is a Savior. He is the Son of the One True God and He wants to reconcile them. Go and baptize them in My Name and teach them to follow all that I have commanded. Jesus added that His followers would do this by His power through the Holy Spirit.

It is by the sacred blood of Christ that we are made holy in God's eyes. It is by His life and death that we are forgiven in God's eyes. It is by God's grace and wisdom that Christ was sent to lavish on us the privilege of being one of His own.

Sealed by the power and the promise of the Holy Spirit we can never lose His love. God orchestrated every instance of His epic redemption using the folly and the joy of man. So that in the fullness of time every man, woman, child, Jew, Greek and foreigner would have an opportunity to know the One True God. Through faith in Christ we are promised an eternity with our heavenly Father who redeemed us from sin and eternal death (Ephesians 1:7-12).

To bring Christ as a perfect sacrifice in the epic redemption, God used marriage. God's epic redemption continues. He is not done. There are still people, groups, friends, family members and neighbors who have not heard and believed the message of Jesus Christ. It is my hope that your married lives will continue to reveal God's epic redemption. Two essential couples in the New Testament provide insight in how to live for Christ's revelation after His resurrection.

## Zacharias and Elizabeth

Zacharias and Elizabeth were a godly couple focused on living for God's glory. The Bible says they were blameless when it came to following the commandments of God (Luke 1:6). However, it was unusual that people so good would have gone so long without children. At this time in the Jewish culture, not having kids was considered a curse. It may have been assumed that Elizabeth was barren because of her sin or her parents' sin.

Then it happened. On a very special day, Zacharias was given the unique opportunity to enter the Holy of Holies and burn incense to the Lord. This privilege came to the priest by casting lots. Zacharias won that day and some scholars believe that this was a once-in-a-lifetime opportunity. While Zacharias was burning incense to the Lord, an angel came to him. He told Zacharias that his prayers had been answered. He was going to have a son that would tell the world about the coming Messiah. Zacharias was shocked! So shocked that he asked the angel for proof! Are you kidding me? Why would you ask an angel of the Lord for proof? Somehow, this old temple priest finds the guts to ask an angel to prove his message. Well, the angel delivers proof and a baby. Zacharias will not be able to talk for the next nine months and somehow the baby will be born and receive the name John.

John the Baptist was born. He was faithful with his message of the coming Messiah. He baptized Jewish men and women preparing them for the repentance they would need to receive from the Christ. Zacharias and Elizabeth had an epic purpose for their marriage. They were to have a prophet for a son. We don't know how long John the Baptist's parents lived after he was born. Some believe a small fundamentalist Jewish community near the Dead Sea may have raised him. It is feasible to believe that Zacharias and Elizabeth had an impact on their child. In fact, I believe that was their purpose, not just to bear the child, but also to prepare him for his message of the coming Messiah.

Zacharias and Elizabeth were an epic couple because they were epic parents. New Testament epic couples seek to be godly parents. Part of godly parenting is instilling in your children that they have a purpose from God. Knowing and believing this will help prepare children for a future of temptation, disappointments, and success. Children will learn this mostly from listening and watching their parents. When you begin to live like you have a purpose bigger than money, selfish desires, or gain, children will catch your wisdom.

Many factors promote godly parenting. I want to encourage you to become a student of parenting. Listen to great speakers who have great kids. Find a church that supports families. Read books and pray for wisdom beyond your years. In addition, constantly pray for your son or daughter. Don't pray for small things like NFL contracts and wealthy husbands. Pray for big things for your children like knowing Christ as Savior at a young age, realizing their divine purpose, having a respectful heart and desiring for the nations to know Christ. Then ask God to give you the wisdom to raise such a child.

Like Zacharias and Elizabeth, parenting begins before kids are born. The habits and priorities you have now will be highlighted when you have kids. Don't wait until kids come to have a relationship with God. Begin now living for His glory and discovering His divine purpose for your life and marriage. Live out His commandments as if you believe He will be faithful to provide, protect, bless and love you no matter what your earthly circumstances tell you. These are hard lessons to learn with the eyes of a teenager watching you. Learn them now and begin your legacy for God's glory.

## Mary and Joseph

The epic is about Jesus. All of history and creation's order has led up to one specific preplanned and ordained perfect moment—the birth of the Messiah Jesus Christ. God wanted His son to come in the form of a man to become the perfect sacrifice for all of humanity. Scripture attests to Jesus being both God and man. He didn't move in and out of humanity and divinity like a phantom. He didn't come to earth like a ghost only to be removed before suffering. Jesus came to the earth as God in the flesh. He felt pain, He had emotions, He was tempted and He was perfectly holy.

In order for Jesus to be all God and all man, He had to be born of a woman. Scripture prophesied and taught that Jesus was conceived by the Holy Spirit and was born of the Virgin Mary. Thus, Jesus was divine and human. Jesus lived thirty-three years on the earth. One day in a synagogue, Jesus revealed His purpose to His listeners:

*The spirit of the Lord is upon me, because He anointed me to preach the gospel to the poor. He has sent me to proclaim release to the captives, and recovery of sight to the blind, to set free those who are oppressed, to proclaim the favorable year of the Lord (Luke 4:18-19 and Isaiah 61:1-2a).*

It should not surprise us that Jesus did exactly as He said He would. He preached to the financially and spiritually poor about the glory of the coming Kingdom of God. He released men and women victims of spiritual captivity. Men who were held captive to wealth and legalism and women who were prostitutes were freed and forgiven by the ministry of Jesus. Jesus gave the physically and the spiritually blind sight with His instruction and grace. Those who were oppressed by religion or by demons were set free by the grace offered in the message and sacrifice of Christ. The "year of favor" was the year Jesus died for all of humanity on the cross.

As I said early on, the entire Bible is about Jesus. God has been blazing the trail and setting the stage for the arrival of His Son. Jesus is the star of the epic. For some reason God decided to use marriage. He didn't have to. Mary was a virgin. She obviously didn't need a husband. It was essential that Jesus was both God and man, so there was no way He was going to be conceived naturally. In fact, Joseph was so faithful to his walk with God that he almost left Mary for getting pregnant before they were married. It was a disgrace to both of them because he knew he didn't have anything to do with the pregnancy. In addition to the miraculous conception, Jesus never addressed Joseph as His father. He always referred to God as His Father. God didn't need Joseph to impregnate Mary or to father Jesus. What did God need with Mary's husband Joseph?

The Bible tells its readers that God sent an angel to Joseph to tell him that his wife was carrying the son of God and he should not to be concerned with her faithfulness. God told Joseph that he was to continue with the engagement and wed Mary. Joseph followed God, married his pregnant wife and kept her a virgin until after Jesus was born. Joseph was a follower of God. After Jesus was born, an angel appeared to Joseph again. This time he told Joseph to take his family to Egypt to flee from King Herod. Joseph believed the messenger of God and immediately left for Egypt. After Herod died God uses an angel to tell Joseph that it was safe to return to Israel. Joseph believed and returned to Israel. As Joseph was traveling, though, he became fearful when he heard that Herod's son took his place as ruler of Judea. Therefore, an angel came to Joseph a fourth time and told him to go to a little town near the coast in the foothills of Galilee called Nazareth. Jesus was born of a virgin in Bethlehem, came out of Egypt and was known as Jesus the Nazarene. All of these characteristics and more were prophesied hundreds of years before Jesus Christ's birth.

The question remains, why was Mary married to Joseph? The accounts of the angels appearing to Joseph are found in the Gospel of Matthew. The Gospel of Luke sheds more light on Joseph's role in the epic of Christ. Eight days after Jesus was born, Joseph did exactly what every good, pious, Jewish man does with his first son. On the eighth day, Joseph took Jesus to the temple to have Him named, circumcised, and presented to the Lord. This was commanded to Abraham concerning Isaac and all his descendants. At the temple, Joseph offered a poor

Jewish family's sacrifice of two turtle doves and two pigeons to the Lord for the life of his first-born son. After these things were done, some saw and believed that Jesus was the Messiah. Joseph took his family and returned home to Nazareth. It was there that the Bible says Jesus grew in strength, grace and wisdom from God.

Twelve years later Joseph took his family to Jerusalem to participate in the Passover. This festival celebrated the exodus from Egypt and God delivering Israel from captivity. From these passages, we see that the family unit was essential to fulfilling Jewish customs and commandments.

From these two Gospel accounts, we gain a better understanding of why Joseph was married to Mary. First, we have seen that God has ordained and proposed marriage to bring Jesus into the world. Marriage is God's perfect and pure idea. He proposed that His Son would come into the world with an intact family. The family is one of God's most basic institutions. It was through the family that God revealed His epic and shaped His people. Family is extremely important to God.

Secondly, we see that Joseph clearly provides spiritual leadership for his family. God guided Joseph to safety and used him to help fulfill the prophecies spoken about the Christ in the Old Testament. In addition to protecting his family, Joseph is used to fulfill the requirements of the Lord regarding first-born sons. Joseph is an essential ingredient to Jesus having a complete intact godly family. This is what God wanted for Jesus.

From Mary and Joseph we learn that an Epic Marriage leads to an epic family. Plainly, we see that Joseph was the leader of his household. God has proposed that the man will be the spiritual leader of the home God has entrusted to him. God would have protected Jesus no matter what. If He had to, God would have told Mary to leave town and would have empowered Mary to make the Jerusalem treks by herself. All these events would have taken place because it was prophesied.

God is not done with marriage. God has a purpose for marriage. Marriage is a God- designed and blessed institution. Its importance is perfectly illustrated when Jesus was born into the arms of a married couple. Marriage was and is essential to the revelation of Christ. Adam and Eve before the fall of humanity and Mary and Joseph at the birth of Christ are a testimony of the epic purpose of marriage and family.

## Epic Marriage Then and Now

We have seen from previous chapters that an Epic Marriage is focused on portraying Christ and not human needs. With Adam and Eve, before the temptation and sin in the Garden of Eden, God created the perfect marriage on His principles. After the fall, God proclaimed that He would use marriage to write the epic of His son's birth.

Abraham and Sarah taught us that faith in God's provision and will was essential to having a marriage focused on Christ and His revelation. Isaac and Rebekah allowed us to see that we must break free from generational baggage and imperfect ideas about marriage if we hope to live out its epic purpose. Moses and Zipporah revealed the essential ingredient of a growing godly wife. A wife is not a passive part of marriage. She is an essential protective ingredient that can help propel a marriage to epic proportions.

Ruth and Boaz showed us that a husband's surrender to God and spiritual leadership in the home is a priority to God's epic purpose for marriage. David and Bathsheba and Hosea and

Gomer revealed the honest reality that sin can be present in marriage. However, we also learned that if you are repentant to your spouse and to God, He can also use a gracious spouse to better portray His abundant mercy and grace despite our sins. Thus, forgiveness is essential to living out your epic purpose in marriage. We concluded with Zachariah and Elizabeth and Mary and Joseph. Both couples were faithful to God and both were key to His epic purpose. Mary and Joseph revealed that the epic continues into the twenty-first century. Even with the final outcome of Christ's birth, death and resurrection, God is not done with marriage.

As we come to the end of a chapter in God's epic, we begin a new chapter on living out the Epic Marriage of God. In the pages that follow, we will consider a letter from the Apostle Paul where he addresses marriage. I hope to provide for you handles by which you grasp the simple purpose of your marriage. In addition, I hope to give you tools to achieve all that God has purposed for your marriage. Your marriage will find its ultimate satisfaction when both of you agree to continue the epic of Christ as God has intended for your marriage.

## Discussion Questions with Your Spouse or Small Group

*How else does God use families in this world?*
*How many children do you plan to have?*
*What will be the priorities of your parenthood?*
*After reading the first section of* Epic Marriage *what couples do you most identify with? What areas of your marriage need the most work?*

# Chapter 10
# Oneness

*For this reason a man will leave his father and mother and be united to his wife, and the two will become one flesh. This is a profound mystery—but I am talking about Christ and the church (Ephesians 5:31-32 [NIV]).*

Two times in my life I have experienced oneness. The first time I was nineteen years old and involved in an organization called Young Life. On a ski trip to Beaver Creek, Colorado, I surrendered my life to Christ and became one with Jesus. Young Life reaches out to high school students who are not Christians. That included most of my high school so all my friends and I went to Young Life on Monday nights. Our Young Life leader was cool. Any adult who takes a legitimate interest in teenagers is eventually cool. Robert was a great guy. He had a Suburban, he was a wealthy bachelor, he played guitar, and he cared about us enough to take us to lunch and give us attention at social events. He always made my friends and I feel like we were the most important people in his life. Robert had something else unique that was magnetic to us. He had purity. There was something very clean about Robert. I could not quite figure it out until that night in Colorado.

Robert asked me if I wanted to hang out (it was the early '90s) with him in the hotel lobby after curfew. Late that night,

Robert and I played guitar and talked about whatever (probably music since that was all I was consumed with back then) in the lobby. Eventually, Robert told me that God sent Jesus into the world to die on the cross so I could be forgiven for my sins and have a relationship with God. I had been looking for God for a long time. I knew He existed, but I just didn't know how to find Him. Something about the way Robert talked about God and Jesus coupled with the way he lived his life made me think he was right. That night Robert asked me if I wanted to become a Christian. Before I could answer, he said, "I want you to think about it; it will change your life. Go up to your bunk and think about it tonight. If you decide to become a Christian, tell Jesus you are sorry for all your sins, that you want Him to be Lord of your life and that you love Him. Let me know in the morning what you decide." I did just as Robert asked and that night I became one with God.

I was not perfect after that night. As a matter fact, I got worse before I got good at Christianity. I still struggle with sin, but there is one thing that has never changed. Since that night, I have been one with God. When He sees me, He sees the righteousness of His Son. He sees one of His children and He sees a soul in which He dwells. I always have oneness with God, but I experience oneness with God when I live the way He has asked me to live. When I fail to strive and labor for godliness, I feel distant from God. We are still one, but I am not experiencing oneness with Him. I don't feel close to Him. My soul is lonely, my spirit is depressed and I miss out on hearing His voice, feeling His touch and knowing His presence. St. Augustine shared in his confessions what he felt when he chose to live in a way opposite of God:

*Behold my heart, O God, behold my heart, which you had pity on when it was in the bottomless pit. Let this heart of mine tell you what it sought there, that I should be evil for naught, and that my sin should have no cause but sin itself. It was foul, and I loved it; that is, I loved my own perishing, I loved my own fault—not that for which I committed the fault, but that the fault itself. Foul soul, leaving security with you and leaping down into destruction, seeking nothing through shame but the shame itself![18]*

St. Augustine recognized the stench of a soul that is not experiencing the oneness of God. It feels empty and uninhabitable. Yet, God still inhabits our souls in seasons of sinfulness. Now that I have experienced oneness with God, I want to live as one with the Father every day. I know I am not perfect and I won't be until I am with Him in eternity, but for now I want strive and labor to live as one with Him.

## The Second One

The second time I became one with someone was when I was twenty-five years old in Waco, Texas. I met a girl almost two years earlier. She was so beautiful she was intimidating. She gripped me with her countenance. Like a confused little dog that chases a jogger down the road to protect its front yard, I didn't know if I was supposed to run from her or run after her. I had never felt this way about any woman before. I knew if I could convince this girl to date me, I would keep her and never let her go. Six months after we started dating, I asked her to marry me. Nine months later in the sacredness of June, Angie and I were standing at the altar exchanging marriage vows. After a long day of tuxedos, dresses, pictures, and family members I didn't know I had, Angie and I crawled in to my mom's Oldsmobile and traveled up I-35 to DFW Airport. We enjoyed a nice meal at a five-star restaurant in Arlington then later that night we became one.

All married couples become one the night they consummate their marriage. Some would argue that you become one when you exchange your vows. That's fine. I don't agree and it's not nearly as much fun. Being one means from here on out the purpose of your marriage is to maintain and experience the oneness you have as a couple. Oneness in marriage is not just making love. Experiencing oneness in marriage is having unity, closeness, and an eternal focus. In order for couples to experience oneness, Christ must be at the center of their marriage.

Just like my relationship with Jesus, there are times I don't feel one with Angie. We are not experiencing oneness when our life together is in disharmony. Just like my relationship with Jesus, when I don't feel like I am one with her, I am still one with her. So many couples forget this fact. They think that when the feeling of oneness is missing, the marriage must be bad. As a result, some take steps to end their marriage. They are right that their marriage is bad, but ending it is not the next step. In fact, it is the exact opposite step of what God would have you to do. When oneness is not experienced in marriage, it is a warning sign that something is missing.

When my relationship with God becomes a tool to achieve what is good for my glory, I don't experience oneness with Him. I have found in the Christian life, sometimes God allows for the things I put ahead of Him to go wrong. God will allow the sand I have tried to build my peace on to erode. Then I will wonder where God is. I love Him and I have tried to follow Him. Now where is He when I need Him the most? Luckily, I have never followed my first thought which was that maybe there is no God. When I wake up to faith, like a sailor off course, I find that my heart was so focused on the sand that over time, I moved my foundation from the Rock. The same experience can happen in marriage. Couples can be so focused on what they think marriage should be that they forget marriage is about the Rock, not the sand.

## Clarifying Oneness

Oneness. Webster defines it as "the state of being unified, whole, or in harmony. The state of being one in number." In Christianity, oneness is a state of being, established by a covenant. No matter what, you are one with Jesus after your conversion and you are one with your spouse after consummation. My goal is for you to experience oneness in marriage. In fact, it was Paul's goal as well. Paul knew that couples who experience oneness could live the most effective lives for reflecting Christ. Since reflecting Christ is a purpose of an Epic Marriage, experiencing oneness with one another should be your first priority.

It is not difficult to know what it takes to experience unity, harmony and wholeness with each other. It is the theme of most marriage conferences. Discover each other's needs, have good communication skills, date your spouse, have intimacy, and so on. These things are important and there is a wealth of great material on these concepts in your local Christian bookstore. The problem is that those books and conferences only address the symptoms and not the problem. My goal and the goal of Scripture is that you will experience spiritual oneness with each other in order that you may reflect the relationship Christ has with His church. The next few chapters will be directed at fixing the problem of most marriages, not the symptoms.

Experiencing spiritual oneness is the harmony you experience in marriage when both you and your spouse are chasing God with equal intensity. As a result, you have both made a decision to put God at the center of your lives. The byproduct is a marriage experiencing the spiritual oneness that you already have.

## Achieving Oneness

The first ingredient of spiritual oneness is having a relationship with Jesus Christ. Spiritual oneness is impossible if both of you are not growing Christians. I think non-believers can have functioning, happy marriages, but since marriage is God's idea, only Christians can fully experience what God has intended for them in marriage.

Having a relationship with Christ is key to the second ingredient to oneness which is an agreed-upon decision that Christ is going to be the center of your marriage. This is a practical conversation you need to have with each other. You may need to ask each other, "What is our marriage about?" or "When ----- is not working, I don't want to be married to you anymore." Is there one thing in your marriage that your unity is dependent upon? If so, Christ is not the center of your marriage. We will discuss more on this in just a moment.

If Jesus is Lord of your lives and you have both agreed to make Jesus the center of your marriage, then the third ingredient may still be difficult, but logical. Both you and your spouse need to agree that whatever God says about marriage, family and life is true. Simply put, believe God and the Bible and make it your goal in marriage to live by His principles. This is not a difficult conclusion, but so many couples struggle with this point. They will enter marriage as Christians. They want to make Jesus the center of their marriage, but the third step is the most important step and it is the one that usually gets ignored.

I believe couples sometimes don't take the third step of living by God's principles because they want it all. The third step is all about surrender. Surrender your needs, desires and expectations about marriage to the Lord. Couples want God to be on their side, but when it comes time to choose between the new car or the tithe, they choose the new car. When it comes time to choose saying bitter things towards to your spouse or forgiveness, bitterness is chosen. Sabbath worship versus day at the lake, you choose day at the lake (nothing wrong with a Sunday at the lake, but if it consistently takes the place of worshiping with a community of believers, your marriage is not centered on Christ). How you choose to use your family's resources, time, and emotions are all indicators of what or Who is at the center of your marriage.

## Oneness Killers

When we mistake marriage for a tool that is solely meant to meet physical needs, support future plans for ministry, wealth or success, we begin to put desires at the center of the marriage. When temporal desires are first in marriage, the marriage is no longer focused on what God has eternally proposed for marriage. As a result, couples begin to miss out on experiencing oneness and the purposes God has for their marriage. This causes relationship chaos. Communication lines come crashing down. Subtle nonverbal clues are missed. Little decisions become major tensions. Nobody's needs are met and home becomes the last place you want to be. In addition, you are not living out one of the God-ordained purposes of your marriage which is to experience oneness that reveals Christ.

As I said earlier, the way we know if we are struggling with placing desires first is by asking ourselves a simple question. "When ----- is not working, do I still want to be married to my wife or husband?" In other words, what causes you to think the worst about your marriage? The root to this answer is *your* purpose of marriage. Let's take a closer look.

Some spouses (mostly men) think that the sole purpose of their marriage is to meet their need for sex. They are right in believing that God has ordained marriage to meet this need. Paul warns the married couples in Corinth not to deprive each other from sex unless it is mutually agreed upon for a season of prayer. That is not the only purpose of your marriage though. The fact of the matter is sexual fulfillment is not possible without first fulfilling the main purpose of marriage. When oneness is missing, making love lacks its intended fulfillment. Without first experiencing oneness, sex in marriage will only meet physical needs. God knows this, which is why there is a greater purpose for your marriage that allows making love to meet deeper needs.

Some spouses think marriage should help propel them to greater career heights. This usually plays out with the wife at home and the husband working ridiculous hours resulting in relationship neglect. That was his or her expectation of marriage. She will stay home, clean and rear the children, and he will work hard, make a lot of money and climb the corporate latter. As soon as the needs at the home become so great that he can't take care of both his career and his home, a man could consider leaving his family for his career. There is nothing wrong with hard work and there is nothing wrong with staying home with the children. Sometimes life is a little off balance and we have to cheat some family time to make ends meet or to keep a boss happy. But your marriage is not about your career or the money you make. If you are cheating on your family at work, you need to find a way out quick! Never cheat on your family for your job. They are the most important lives God has entrusted to you. It is your first responsibility to take care of them and to ensure a godly legacy (check out *Choosing to Cheat* by Andy Stanley).

A benefit to oneness with your spouse is the greatest tool for producing a godly legacy. When your days are coming to an end, the square footage of your retirement home will not be nearly as important as having kids who love you and who are regularly experiencing oneness with God and their spouse. This won't happen while you are at work.

Wives can struggle with the idea that marriage is meant to give them a family. God clearly tells us that couples are to be fruitful and multiply. It is a glorious gift to bring a son or daughter into the world. The idea that this little guy or girl is mine to love and rear to help better the world and extend God's renown is very fulfilling. If the kids go bad, or if kids aren't a possibility, do you think you shouldn't be married? I hope not. My mind is flooded with great couples (evangelical-history-changing couples) who for whatever reason don't have kids or had a kid who freely chose to not follow God. God is using their surrendered lives for incredible things. I believe that as parents, it is our job to rear a God-fearing spiritually healthy legacy, but it is not the sole purpose of marriage.

Oneness-killers exist in your relationship with God as well. We see them when we think God should perform a miracle based on our merit or good work. Thankfully, God's love is not dependent on my merit, but I still desire Him to bless me when I follow His Word. It is important to understand that we are not to follow God for the good that may result in our lives. We are to follow God because of the ultimate Glory it will give Him with our lives. This is surrender; giving up your glory for His.

When God does not do the things I expect Him to do because I am a Christian, I sometimes think about turning from my faith decision or calling. When I started tithing and my car broke down, I got mad at God for letting this happen. When I chose to be honest with someone about an accident and I was not spared the consequences, I was mad at God for not helping me. When I worked hard and prayed harder, but God didn't seem to bless the things I did, I thought God must not care about me. When I was faithful to a vision God had given me for a ministry at church and someone else got the glory for it, I get mad at God because that was my time for glory and not theirs. I think those things because my Christianity is sometimes based on my expectation that serving God will get me wealth, health, success and blessings, when really my Christianity is about reaching the lost, training the found and making God's name great. When I put Christ at the center of my relationship with Him (that sounds funny, but that's what we need to do) I find that I experience oneness with Him. Nothing can take away the deep oneness a man or woman has with God or their spouse. Deep spiritual oneness with God and your spouse begins with surrender.

## Epic Oneness

Paul writes in Ephesians, "For this reason a man will leave his father and mother and be united to his wife, and the two will become one flesh. This is a profound mystery—but I am talking about Christ and the church." He is telling married couples that the greater purpose of their relationship is to reveal Jesus Christ. When couples put Jesus at the center of their relationship, they experience epic oneness. When oneness is experienced, Christ is revealed. We must be living in oneness with our spouse if we are going to reveal Christ in our marriage.

With oneness in marriage, we create our own epic, revealing Jesus. Like Adam and Eve, Abraham and Sarah, or David and Bathsheba, our epic story of Christ is filled with brokenness, unmet needs, and past hurts. In the midst of life's struggles of marriage there is an unexplainable surrender and joyful passion for each other. Your story contains events that would end most relationships, but because your marriage is orbiting around Christ, you persevere and are now stronger. Those who watch will only wonder where the help comes from. How did they make it through that? Would our marriage have survived those circumstances? If Christ is your center then the answer would be yes.

In the chapters to come I hope to shed a little light on what I have come to find to be the first step in oneness. For me oneness with Angie and keeping Jesus at the center of our marriage has been a journey. I don't think I have all the answers and I don't know if I ever will. I do know this: When I do things God's way, no matter what happens, I know He will get the glory for it. Not only that, but He will also make me more like His Son through the journey. So I would like for you to join me in a marital step of faith. The step begins by believing in Christ as Savior, committing to making Him the center of your marriage, and surrendering to His commands knowing. You may have unfulfilled expectations and desires. Funny thing is either way you will have unmet needs and unfulfilled expectations. At least this way you will know your marriage is centered on Christ and that He will get the glory for your sufferings.

## Discussion Questions with Your Spouse or Small Group

*Describe what it feels like to experience oneness with God.*

*Describe what it feels like to experience oneness with your spouse.*

*If it is not Jesus, what is your marriage centered on?*

*What changes can you make today to center your marriage on Christ?*

# Chapter 11
# A Wife's Role in an Epic Marriage

Every marriage has a purpose. Please forgive my repetition. It just happens to be the point of the book and I don't want you to miss it. The purpose of your marriage is two things. The first purpose of marriage is to have babies. As we saw with Adam and Eve, God commanded them to be fruitful and multiply. Having descendants is what began the Epic Marriage. So have babies. If you love Jesus, want to actively participate in rearing your children to follow Christ in grace, truth and love, then have a lot of kids! Really, we need more committed parents and godly children. When you come to the point in life when you want nothing more than to propel someone deeper in his or her relationship with God than you have ever gone, but you're still close enough to show the way, then get busy and multiply.

That's not all. According to God there is one more purpose for marriage—to be a reflection of the kind of relationship one can have with Him through Christ. This is the Epic Marriage. Kids don't make an Epic Marriage. They are great and Angie and I want a ton! What your marriage reflects is what makes it epic. The point of all these pages has been to show you that from the very beginning, God has been about revealing His son through marriage literally and figuratively. Now that Christ has come, this purpose has not changed. God still wants to use your marriage to reveal His Son.

As we discussed in the last chapter, it is through oneness that Christ is revealed in your marriage. We added that oneness is experienced through a relationship with Jesus Christ, an agreement to make Him the center of your marriage and to follow what God's Word says about marriage. In this chapter, we will look at the wife's role according to God's Word. A bride's role is essential in creating a marital environment of oneness. In the next chapter, we will consider man's essential role in oneness in marriage.

## An Epic Wife

*and be subject to one another in the fear of Christ. Wives, be subject to your own husbands, as to the Lord. For the husband is the head of the wife, as Christ also is the head of the church, He Himself being the Savior of the body. But as the church is subject to Christ, so also the wives ought to be to their husbands in everything (Ephesians 5:21-24).*

A wife's role in an Epic Marriage is to play the role of the church. Church is a place where you go to be made holy by the grace of God. Church is about joining with a community of like-minded believers and worshiping a holy God. It is about being forgiven and not being perfect. It is about building others up, not just soaking the message in. The church has received an amazing gift in Christ. His blood redeems us so that we can have an eternal relationship with our Heavenly Father. We are special in God's eyes as we are uniquely gifted and empowered to serve Him. This is the church, and the gates of Hell cannot stand against her. Nothing can separate her from the love of her Savior.

When a wife enters into a marriage relationship she is called by God to play the role of the church. Her husband is called to play the role of Christ (we will get to that, some of you may be thinking he has further to go if that's the case...).

The Scripture defines the role of the church is a role of submission to Christ. Has any one word caused more division in the past couple hundred years? Denominations, loyal friends, and lovers have split because of this one word, "submission." The word submission in the Greek means, "submit." It does not matter how we say it or cut it, "submit" means to submit.

It is worth pointing out that in the Greek text the series of verses that discuss submission of wives begins with submitting to one another. I think Paul wanted to make it clear that a wife's submission does not lessen her in the eyes of God and he wanted to reinforce that there is no Greek, Jew, Gentile, male or female in Christ. All are equally important and equally His. The Bible is not saying that women are less because they are called to submit to their husbands. The role of submission is simply their God-ordained role in marriage. This does not mean a wife is a spiritual weakling or a special project for man to fix. It just means that a woman's role in marriage is to let her husband lead.

Why would God set up such a system? Didn't He know that one day a bunch of Americans would think He was narrow-minded for prescribing such an archaic role? Well, I think He knew that Americans were going to fuss, but He is brilliant. Not only is God brilliant, but He also has your best interests in mind. He knows what a marriage relationship should look like and after all, marriage was His idea. He knows that if we do it His way, we will experience what He wants us to experience— oneness. God knows that your marriage is best when one person is the leader. God has chosen men to fulfill this role. When you chose God, you also chose your roles in marriage.

I became a Christian when I was nineteen years old on a Young Life ski trip. Unlike most new Christians, I had no one to tell when I arrived home. I went home and it was business as usual. I didn't think anyone would care and my dad was not a Christian. So late one night I told my stepmom I had become a Christian. I told her about the whole experience and explained how my life was beginning to change. She began to rekindle her relationship with God about that same time. She started praying a lot and studying her Bible. All the sudden she was the most spiritual person in the house. We went to an Episcopal Church and my dad was supportive of my stepmom, so he went along for the ride. All along, my stepmom was growing in the Lord. As I left for college, I saw something. My dad was still in charge. There was no question about it. He still was in charge of the Werley family. Although my stepmom may have been closer to God, she submitted to my dad's authority. She never pushed Scripture on him. She never used Bible verses as weapons in fights. She simply submitted as she was commanded to do in Scripture.

You may be thinking, *Well she sounds nice and all, but I come from a tough background and I have worked too hard to let some man tell me what and where I should go.* Yeah, I thought you might say that. My stepmom is a first born, strong willed, type-A, logical person. She went to law school at UT and became one of the youngest women partners at her law firm. She is no pushover. She is tough, annoyingly tough, now that I think about it. Despite all her success in the world her relationship with God moved her to submit to my dad at home.

Years later just like the Bible says in I Peter, "In the same way, you wives, be submissive to your own husbands so that even if any of them are disobedient to the word, they may be won without a word by the behavior of their wives" (I Peter

3:1). My dad was won to the Lord because of his wife's submission. Watching this transformation take place changed my life. It was one of the core events of my life. It helped me to believe in the inerrant truth and practicality of God's Word. Now my dad is a conservative Bible-loving Christian. He and my stepmom have for some time felt called to the Episcopal Church to help see it return to its conservative roots and worship the one true living God in spirit and truth. Submission is a beautiful thing and sometimes it even changes lives.

## What if He's Wrong?

Sometimes following God's command to submit will lead you to submit to your husband even when he is wrong. Again, I am not saying you do not have a voice and that you should not speak up in marriage if something is not right or if you have an opinion about something. However, at some point, you will need to physically let go and spiritually hold on!

In most cases throughout Scripture, God protected the people who chose to submit to the people God placed over them. For example, King Saul was hunting King David before he was king. King Saul was David's king. In one scene King Saul goes into a cave to go to the bathroom and as his pants are around his ankles, David and his army are hiding in the cave. David had the perfect opportunity to kill the king. David submitted to the king and did not kill him even though the king was trying to kill David. Later God protects David and he eventually becomes the King of Israel.

Numerous passages speak of this kind of protection. Trust yourself and your family into God's protection. In addition, pray. We all need to pray for our spouses. Pray for God to change his heart, to mold him and to give him wisdom beyond his years. You may be surprised to see what God does when He hears the prayers of a wife actually submitting to her husband.

## When Not to Submit

You never, ever, ever have to submit to do something your husband tells you to do that is clearly against God's commandments in Scripture. Your commitment to God comes before your commitment to your husband. If your husband asks you to steal, kill or break one of God's commandments, you can refuse and run for help if you must. If he asks you to lie, you can refuse. However, if any of these things are happening in your marriage, I want to encourage you to find Biblical Christian counseling immediately. These are dreadful red flags in any relationship.

Secondly, I do not think you have to endanger your health or your physical well being in order to submit to your husband. In other words, if he is abusing you physically, you get yourself out of that house and get some help. Again, find some great Christian counseling and protect your life. You do not have to submit to an abusive spouse. Scripture clearly deals with this subject. I believe God the Father wants you to know His love and live to serve Him. You cannot do that when you are in an abusive relationship. Expose that relationship to the light of God and get yourself and your family in a safe place.

## How Should You Submit?

The Bible says wives are to submit to their husbands as an act of worship to God (Ephesians 5:22). Your submission is a blessing to your husband. God is using you to bless your husband. In marriage, submission is not something that can be demanded. It is a gift given by a godly wife. It is a gift of a peaceful relationship. It is the gift of allowing your husband to protect you and care for your needs. It is a gift of devotion and commitment to one man for the rest of your life. Submission is a gift of love that you give your husband and while worshiping God.

In the same way, the church submits to God. God has given the church the gift of free will. Love demanded is not love at all. Therefore, the church chooses freely to love God, to allow Him to lead her, to protect her, to serve her, and to make her better through her submission. When the church does this, she worships God. It is an offering of love when we submit to God and allow His Word and His heart for us to dictate our lives. When the church submits, she proclaims to the nations that there is no god before our God. He is the one true holy Lord God almighty. Submission to your God, king or husband proclaims this glorious truth.

## Be a Church

The church is made up of many different types of people with different qualities and characteristics. God loves each one of us and He created us just the way we are. God is not surprised by emotion. He has never told us not to be emotional. God is not surprised by our opinions about how things should be. God made wives with wisdom and an incredible capacity to love and cherish others. He also gave them a deep desire for profound solid friendships and for a solid and intimate relationship with a great man. Be you. Speak your mind in gentleness. Allow the peace of God to reign in your heart so that when you address your husband he feels honored, cherished, and lucky to have you for a wife. Be so gentle that he wants to come home from work. Speak positive words into his life and watch him begin to live up to them. Allow the Holy Spirit to do the work of fixing him. Sit back and enjoy the oneness you will discover hiding beneath the fights, competitiveness, and pride.

Ladies, when you choose to play the role of the church in your marriage, you are epic wives. This will send a powerful message to anyone watching your relationship (and people are watching). Your friends will wonder why you do what you do, and why your marriage has the peace that it has. People will notice, people will talk, and you will have nothing to attribute it to except for the inspiration of Christ and His church.

Proverbs 31 speaks of a woman who is epic. She is wise and gracious and powerful. She is generous. She is resourceful. She works inside and outside the home. She prioritizes her family first. She looks good. She honors her husband and she has a great reputation. Look for these qualities and pray them over your life. Allow the model of this godly woman be your goal as a wife.


*A good woman is hard to find, and worth far more than diamonds.*

*Her husband trusts her without reserve, and never has reason to regret it.*

*Never spiteful, she treats him generously all her life long.*

*She shops around for the best yarns and cottons, and enjoys knitting and sewing.*

*She's like a trading ship that sails to faraway places and brings back exotic surprises.*

*She's up before dawn, preparing breakfast for her family and organizing her day.*

*She looks over a field and buys it, then, with money she's put aside, plants a garden.*

*First thing in the morning, she dresses for work, rolls up her sleeves, eager to get started.*

*She senses the worth of her work, and is in no hurry to call it quits for the day.*

*She's skilled in the crafts of home and hearth, diligent in homemaking.*

*She's quick to assist anyone in need, and reaches out to help the poor.*

*She doesn't worry about her family when it snows; their winter clothes are all mended and ready to wear.*

*She makes her own clothing, and dresses in colorful linens and silks.*

*Her husband is greatly respected when he deliberates with the city fathers.*

*She designs gowns and sells them, brings the sweaters she knits to the dress shops.*

*Her clothes are well-made and elegant, and she always faces tomorrow with a smile.*

*When she speaks, she has something worthwhile to say, and she always says it kindly.*

*She keeps an eye on everyone in her household, and keeps them all busy and productive.*

*Her children respect and bless her; her husband joins in with words of praise:*

*"Many women have done wonderful things, but you've outclassed them all!"*

*Charm can mislead and beauty soon fades. The woman to be admired and praised is the woman who lives in the Fear-of-God.*

*Give her everything she deserves! Festoon her life with praises! (Proverbs 31:10-31, [The Message]).*

# Discussion Questions with Your Spouse or Small Group

*What emotions do you feel when you hear or read the word submit? Why?*

*Did you (wife) struggle with submitting to authority as a young lady? Is that struggle still with you now?*

*What are some immediate ways you can submit to your husband?*

*What fears do you have about submitting to your husband?*

# Chapter 12
# Epic Husband

## Manhood

Who taught you about manhood? For the majority of us men, our fathers taught us what it means to be a man. It is a natural fit. He is the most prominent man in our life and we see his example every day. It would be only natural for us to learn what we know about being a man from our dads. This is good and I believe this is the way God intended for young boys to grow into strong men. The problem is that some dads miss the boat on teaching their sons the most important things of life. I believe that it is mainly because they do not know what the most important things in life are.

I know this is true and present in the church because I have heard what dads value teaching their sons. In addition, I have seen young men make bad decisions regarding the most important things in life. Years ago, when I was a youth pastor at my first church I was talking to a college professor who also served as a deacon. He was proud of the fact that he could walk his son through an engine overhaul over the phone. He felt like teaching his son how to repair the family car and work with his hands was his job as a dad. Somehow, these skills would propel him into a glorious future. Dads want to teach their sons how to hunt, work, sell, and sometimes fight. With the exception of fighting (Jesus would not approve...) these are all fine things to teach a son and they help to establish a common ground between a father and a son.

For years, my dad and I worked out together. When I entered high school, we began the habit of waking up at five in the morning and driving downtown to the Fort Worth Club and lifting weights together. I had my own personal trainer and really enjoyed the spa/hot tub before school. My dad taught me how to change the oil in my car and taught me how to work. I painted our lake house one winter. We planted two pear trees in the front yard. That was when he taught me that if you pour a little beer down to the roots it helps them grow faster (I wouldn't bother testing that scientifically). In fact, beer fixed everything. A little beer on a hurt arm after you fell on your bike, all better. Yep, beer is important to have around the house for bruises and trees. My dad taught me to respect people, to manage my money, to work hard in athletics, and to work harder in school.

Maybe your dad was like mine. He was good. He was hands-on for the most part, but he failed at one task. He is not held responsible in my heart because he was not a Christian when he was rearing me, but my dad failed to teach me how to have a relationship with God. The most important relationship you will ever have is a relationship with God. Everything about being a man depends on knowing God. Having godly wisdom, strong ethical standards, deep life-changing prayer, and worshiping God all depend on knowing God. Yet so many dads are more concerned with teaching the practical they forget the important spiritual things of life. It's okay. Practical is easier. We can put our hands on it. Practical has tangible results, but we are all spiritual. Deep inside every man there is something spiritual occurring and in the silent, scary, haunting and profound moments you wonder, *What will we do then?* That is when a relationship with God is crucial.

Before my son was born, I bought him a Bible. In about sixteen, maybe eighteen years, I will give it to him. It depends on his spiritual maturity. In the meantime, it has become my devotional Bible. Every morning that I get up to spend time in God's Word, I read his Bible with a pen in hand. I plan to read and write in the entire Bible before I give it to him. I write things like; "I have been praying this for you..." "This verse spoke to me today because..." I also give him insight in what I believe about God and humanity based on the Scripture read that day. It has been an incredible experience. It is like having a deep conversation with my one-year-old every morning. I love it. On the front page, I wrote him a little note. It says a lot of stuff, but in regards to our present context it says, "Son, as your father, I hope to teach you how to have the two most important relationships you will ever have. I want to teach you through this book how to relate to your God who loves you very much and with my life, actions and words, I want to show you how to love your wife like I love your mom."

The first job of a father is not to teach their sons how to work on cars or make a living. The first job of a dad is to teach their sons how to know God and the second is to teach them how to love their wives. Both are taught and both are caught. This requires that you live out an honest, pure, passionate relationship with your God and your wife.

I hope to help you begin to make a shift in the way you express love and leadership towards your wife and your home. In previous chapters, we learned that for men to be leaders in the home they must first be worshipers of God. From Boaz we learned we need to be followers of God as we patiently wait and do His will. In this chapter, we will learn from the Apostle Paul the final ingredient to epic manhood loving as Christ loves. Jesus taught us how to relate to our God. Paul adds that in teaching us how God loves us, Jesus taught husbands how to love their wives:

*Husbands, love your wives, just as Christ also loved the church and gave Himself up for her, so that He might sanctify her, having cleansed her by the washing of water with the word, that He might present to Himself the church in all her glory, having no spot or wrinkle or any such thing; but that she would be holy and blameless. So husbands ought also to love their own wives as their own bodies. He who loves his own wife loves himself; for no one ever hated his own flesh, but nourishes and cherishes it, just as Christ also does the church, because we are members of His body. FOR THIS REASON A MAN SHALL LEAVE HIS FATHER AND MOTHER AND SHALL BE JOINED TO HIS WIFE, AND THE TWO SHALL BECOME ONE FLESH. This mystery is great; but I am speaking with reference to Christ and the church (Ephesians 5:25-32).*

When a wife submits to a husband, the marriage is not epic until the husband lives out his end of the God-given role for marriage. The wife is epic, but the marriage is still not focused on Christ. Many of you are married to epic wives and you have never stepped up to be an epic husband. The time is now. If you begin to live with your wife the way God has called you, you will not only have incredible oneness, but you will be accurately reflecting the relationship God has with His church.

Read, reflect, journal, highlight and ponder the next few pages. Begin making the shift from a self-centered relationship to a Christ-centered relationship with your wife. I must warn you that this lifestyle change may be the most difficult thing you ever do. It is the everyday choice of choosing your hobbies or your wife, choosing work or your wife, time off for you or time off with your wife. This commitment will change everything. It will be the best decision you ever made. In ten, fifteen, twenty years, you will thank this little book because your marriage will not be dry, wounded and purposeless. Instead, it will be full of life and beginning to seeing the fruit of choosing to have a marriage the way God intended.

## The Willful Lover

*Husbands love your wives, just as Christ also loved the church and gave Himself up for her, so that He might sanctify her...(Ephesians 5:25a).*

The first shift most men will have to make will come in the way they view and live out love. Love in America is tossed around and beaten by a slew of diamond commercials and sitcoms. Most of us men have never seen how to love like a man. Paul says our example of love comes from none other than the Son of Love, Jesus Christ.

Your leadership in the home is first being the leader in loving. Your wife and children should have the opportunity to submit to your love. We typically think our leadership begins with our earned authority and our wives should submit to that hard-earned authority. Culturally, we are taught that leadership comes with strength and discipline. Biblically, men don't earn leadership in the home. They are commanded to be the leaders of the home. Not only are we commanded to lead our families, we are also commanded to lead like Christ leads the church in love.

Jesus gave humanity its most incredible illustration of love. I recently heard a sermon by Voddie Baucham on men's leadership in the home where he pointed out that Jesus willfully loved the church.[19] He goes on to make an excellent point that while Jesus was in the Garden of Gethsemane, He did not emotionally desire to die on the cross for the sins of humanity. Nevertheless, Jesus makes a decision of the will: "My Father, if this cannot pass away unless I drink it, Your will be done" (Matthew 26:42).

Jesus showed us in that moment that true love is not about emotions. It is about the will. Men are to lead their families by willfully loving them. Men do this when they make the decision to love their wife no matter how they are feeling about her. It seems more and more often, I am hearing stories of young couples divorcing because they did not feel in love anymore or even worse committing adultery because someone else made them feel special. That is not love. It certainly is not the love of Christ. That is the lie of American pop culture.

Does this mean you don't need to be emotionally drawn to your wife? No, that is not what I am saying. However, when it comes to love, feelings are deceiving. As a matter of fact, you will find that when you begin to willfully love your wife no matter what and stop compromising your love for her with your thoughts and actions, your emotional love will grow deeper for her. God has created you this way. It is the reward of willfully loving someone.

When we willfully love, we become investors in our marriage. I don't do the stock market thing. I am interested in it, but trading online and messing with my mutual funds is not something I have ever dabbled with. I get a statement every quarter letting me know how my 403B is looking, and since I started it six years ago, I take note of what the Dow Jones is doing and what the different presidents say they are going to do about the economy. I have a vested interest in my retirement. In fact, if it was all taken away from me, I would hurt, weep and wonder how I would ever get it back. You could say I have an emotional relationship with my investments. I have a healthy portfolio because I willfully invest a portion of my income into retirement. After 9/11 and the market began to bottom out, I stuck with my investments. When the war in Iraq started and gas prices spiked, I kept investing. When Angie and I started having kids, our income went down, and our expenses went up, but we continued to invest. No matter what, I have tried to make a willful commitment to invest for retirement. I bet 90% of the men reading this book have done the same thing.

If I were to come take your investment away from you, you would get very angry and file a lawsuit against me to put in me in prison for a very long time. You would not say, "It's just green pieces of paper with pictures of dead presidents. I'll get some more." You would be very angry and you would not rest until you got your money back. If this is true, you have an emotional connection with your money.

Marriage is an investment of the will. When you decide to willfully invest love into your marriage no matter what hard times befall you, you will reap the benefits of not only having a deeper emotional connection with your wife, but you will have a marriage that is grounded on the love of Christ. Leadership in the home willfully loves a wife no matter what. Don't be distracted by the dips in the market or the words of someone else. You stay true to your investment. Continue to trust God, love her and know that together you can be all that God has intended for you to be.

## Servant Lover

*...gave Himself up for her, so that He might sanctify her, having cleansed her by the washing of water with the word, that He might present to Himself the church in all her glory, having no spot or wrinkle or any such thing; but that she would be holy and blameless. So husbands ought also to love their own wives as their own bodies (Ephesians 5:25c-27a).*

Paul continues painting the picture of an epic husband. He points out that husbands are to reflect Christ by adding to their willful loving an attitude of service. In the gospels, there are many accounts of the servant's heart of Jesus. The most noted is the foot-washing scene before the Passover and the crucifixion. In that scene as Jesus washes His disciples' feet, he explains to them the significance servant leadership:

*You call Me Teacher and Lord; and you are right, for so I am. If I then, the Lord your Teacher, washed your feet, you also ought to was one another's feet. For I gave you an example that you also should do as I did to you...If you know these things you are blessed if you do them (John 13:13-15 and 16).*

As the Son of God with all the authority of Heaven and Earth behind Him, Jesus washed the dirty, stinky, feet of the disciples. Paul draws us back to this event for our marriage when he writes, "having cleansed her by the washing of water with the word."

This was one of the first principles I learned about marriage. In fact, I tell young single men all the time that if they are not willing to serve a woman for the rest of their lives, then they are not ready to get married. Great leaders serve. Likewise, great husbands are servants.

Paul says our service has a reason. We serve to encourage our wives to be better followers of Christ. So your servant leadership should be devoted to seeing your wife become the best individual for Christ she can be. I am not saying you become a slave to every disposal of your wife. I am saying there will be seasons when you put your needs, desires, and hobbies to the side in order to be a servant to her. It is a complete paradigm shift. This will not be easy, but your position in the home requires it.

As with the wife's submission there are extreme positions when it comes to servant leadership. A wife has just as much to say in a family as the husband does. Her input is of great value and if you have ever attempted to make decisions regarding the family without her input you have discovered this to be true. Submission is not sitting in a corner waiting to be told what to do. Wives submit actively, while the husbands have the responsibility to make the final call if the situation absolutely requires it. The same can be said for a man's servant love. I have seen guys who get pushed around and taken advantage of by their wives. I do not think this is servant love; this is spinelessness.

Being a servant lover is taking care of your wife's needs just as you would take care of your own. I think this is what Paul meant when he said, "So husbands ought also to love their own wives as their own bodies. He who loves his own wife loves himself" (Ephesians 5:28). When you get hungry, you feed yourself. When you get thirsty, you get something to drink. When you get fat, you go work out. If you feel depressed, you try to lift your spirits. A Christ-like husband does this for his wife as well. In other words, you know your wife as well as you know yourself. If she has needs, you try to meet them the best you can.

# A Practical Word for the Epic Husband

Last night as I was writing this chapter, I got very excited. I was almost done with my first book and I was cruising through this chapter. My mind was fresh, the house was quiet, and for some reason words were flowing straight from my soul to the keyboard. Then Angie came into the room. We had already decided that she was going to bed before me because I was going to finish this chapter.

We start talking about ministry and some couples who were not doing so great. One couple in particular was dealing with some major unfaithfulness issues. After we finished talking, I said, "Goodnight, babe."

She replied, "You're coming with me."

I said, "No, remember I am going to finish this chapter tonight." I explained to her how great I was feeling and how I felt like I was in the groove and could not wait to finish. Then I realized she needed me to go to bed with her. We decided early in marriage that healthy couples go to bed together. For years, every night we have tried to go to bed and say prayers together. This was one of those exception nights, I thought. After my realization I said, "Alright, let's get to bed." She felt bad and tried to talk me out of it, but it was too late. I realized she needed me and I wanted to serve her. So ,we went to bed, prayed for that couple and fell asleep.

Writing was a good thing. I was excited about it. I was being productive and everything was in place for me to justify why I needed to stay up late. Sometimes the stories and heartbreaks of ministry can take a toll on a couple in the ministry. So, I stopped what I was doing to serve my wife. The result of my service that morning is our marriage is now stronger, our love is more secure and I might even finish this chapter today.

You may need to rethink some daily habits and decisions that interfere with your wife becoming the best woman for God she can be. You have the most influence in her life regarding her growth in the Lord. Be sure you are a good steward of the authority and influence God has given you in her life. It is a privilege and an honor.

With that said, it is not your job to make your wife holy. I know that is what the Bible says Jesus does for the church, but that means He is doing it for your wife too! So, you're off the hook. You never have to force Scripture on her in a conversation. You do not need to make her have a devotional time every morning. It is not your responsibility to make her go to a Bible Study at church or be part of a woman's ministry. Those are all things she must do by her own free will.

Your job is to pray for your wife's holiness and be sure you don't hinder the process. Prayer has been my most powerful tool when it comes to God working on my wife. Don't get me wrong, Angie has a lot of prayers she's praying over me as well. Instead of getting frustrated at things I wished my wife did differently, I pray for her relationship with God. I pray that God will continue to speak to her heart regarding certain issues. You won't believe it, but it works! I don't have to try and make my wife holy. I can just ask God to do it and then sit back and enjoy the company.

One final thought regarding your motivation for servant and willful love. Notice that when Paul describes the reasons for Christ washing the church, it was to cleanse her. The church was not lovely. We are sinners, yet God loved us enough to send His Son and He continues to sanctify us to make us holy. Jesus did not wait until we earned His love before He gave His love. As husbands, we need to be willing to extend love to our wives even when we think they don't deserve it. She should not submit to you based on your earned respect and you shouldn't love her only when she is loveable. Just as Christ is our Rock, your love needs to be an unwavering rock. Be that rock for your wife and she will become more lovable than you ever imagined. These are the qualities of an epic husband. Go now and love your wife as Christ loves the church.

## Discussion Questions with Your Spouse or Small Group

*Who taught you how to be a man? What did he teach you?*
*What intimidates you (husband) about leading your family?*
*Who is the spiritual leader of your home?*
*How would your leadership help the home?*
*What changes do you need to make immediately to better love and serve your wife?*

# Chapter 13
# Epic Conclusion

I hope you have enjoyed the Epic Marriage. The process of becoming an Epic Marriage is a journey. The best part about the long journey ahead of you is knowing you are seeking God's best together as you discover the purpose of your marriage is to reflect God's epic gift, Jesus Christ. You will not regret applying these Scriptural principles to your marriage.

As you pray and work through these principles, I hope they propel you further into your God-given purpose as a couple. Each couple that reads this book and decides to apply the Epic Marriage to their relationship will discover they want to do more. I hope you will begin to cast vision for your marriage. God is birthing in you a heart for a particular people group, organization, or need in your community. Begin asking yourselves how your marriage can reflect Christ in your current context.

I also want to encourage you to get some tools to further the depth of your oneness. *For Women Only* by Shanti Feldhahn is a must for any married couple. *The Five Love Languages* by Gary Chapman has been a great tool for Angie and me throughout the years. Your spiritual gifts play a big role in how you relate to each other and how God may call you to serve Him as a couple. *Discovering Your God-Given Gifts* by Don and Katie Fortune will help reveal your individual grace gifts to you. As I was proposing this book to different publishers, Voddie Baucham preached his sermon on Love and Marriage to North Point Community Church's singles ministry, 722. You may still be able to order the sermon from the 722 store on-line. It's a motivating series that briefly encapsulates everything the Epic Marriage has aimed to say.

Finally, I hope you enjoy some great epic films. If you want to encourage your marriage, see *A Beautiful Mind* and watch a Zipporah-like wife in an Epic Marriage. *When We Were Soldiers* is a great epic that reveals beautifully what God can do through a couple that is unified in love. Mel Gibson and his wife in the movie are epic in their outreach to their community. *Cinderella Man* is a great example of a willful and servant lover. It is a powerful movie that may change to way you view family for the rest of your life.

Again thank you for reading my book and considering my vision to see every Christian marriage become an Epic Marriage. I pray for you all and I desire God's very best for you as you apply these principles. I hope each of you will enjoy a nice long epic married life. Now go and be epic!

# Quotations and Sources

[1]**Chapter 2**
*iAbout a Boy* © Universal Studios, 2002.
[2] Gordan J. Wenham, *Word Biblical Commentary*, Genesis 1-15 (pg. 69).
[3] *http://www.umm.edu/conjoined_twin/facts.html*, by Noël Holto,. University of Maryland Medical System, Web Site Writer.

**Chapter 3**
[4] Andy Stanley, *Discovering God's Will*, © 2000
[5] Andrew Peterson, "Canaan Bound," from *The Sound of Thunder* CD (2005).

**Chapter 4**
[6] S. Courtney Bicket, Alice Lapray, *The Long Term Impact of Adolescent Risky Behaviors and Family Environment, http://aspe.hhs.gov/hsp/riskybehav01/index.htm, 2006.*
[7] Jennifer Howard, "Little Kid, Big Temper? How to prevent meltdowns and help your child control his emotions." *Parenting Magazine, http://www.parenting.com/parenting/child/article/0,19840,1549594,00.html*

**Chapter 5**
[8] Cindy Crosby, *Marriage Partnership: The Best Sex Survey Ever,* Winter 2004 (49).
[9] Cindy Crosby (49).

[10] Shanti Feldhahn, *For Women Only: What you need to know about the inner lives of men,* Multnomah Publishers, Sisters, Oregon, 2004 (94).
[11] Ibid., 25
[12] Feldhahn (30)
[13] Ibid.
[14] Feldhahn (45)

**Chapter 6**
[15] Robert L. Hubbard Jr., *The New International Commentary on the Old Testament: The Book of Ruth,* William B. Eerdmans Publishing Company, Grand Rapids, MI, 1988 (132).

**Chapter 7**
[16] *http://www.divorcepeers.com/stats31.htm "Anatomy of an Affair," Men's Health: Best Life, Spring/Summer 2003,* Laurence Roy Stains, page 78.
[17] Ibid.

**Chapter 9**
[18] St. Augustine. *The Confessions of St. Augustine,* Modern English Version, by Hal M. Helms, 1986.

**Chapter 10**
[19] Voddie Baucham, *Love and Marriage; Part 2 True Love,* 722 Resources, Alpharetta, GA, 2005.

For more information or resources on Epic Marriage visit: *www.epicmarriage.com.*

Andrew Werley challenges young couples weekly to have an Epic Marriage. If you are interested in hosting Andrew Werley for an emphasis on marriage at your organization or church please contact him: *owner@epicmarriage.com.*